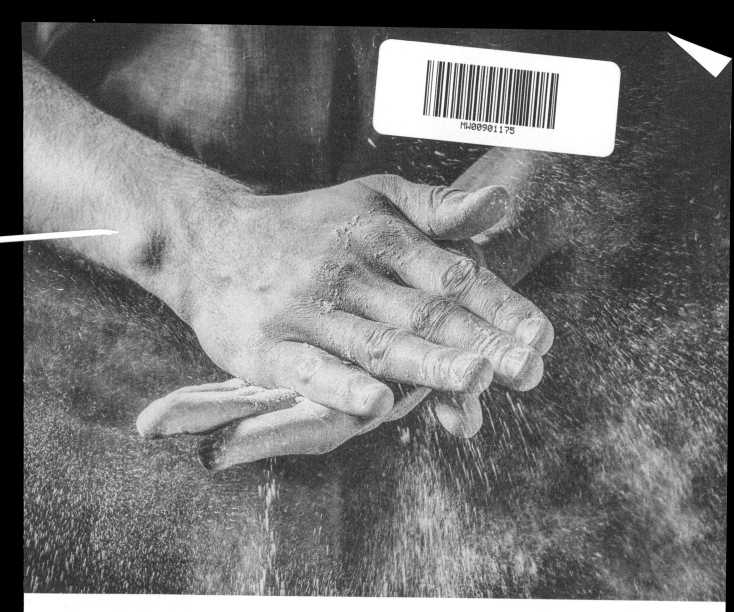

DIABETIC COOKBOOK FOR BEGINNERS

THE BEST EASY AND TASTY RECIPES WITH BALANCED MEALS AND THE RIGHT FOOD COMBINATIONS TO SET UP A CORRECT DIET AND REGAIN HEALTHY BODYWEIGHT.

Cheryl Shea

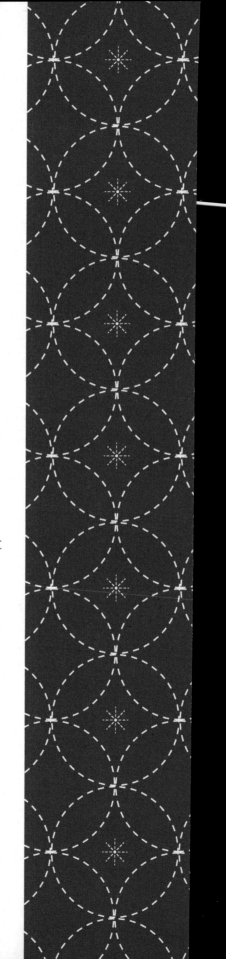

TABLE OF CONTENTS

CHAPTER 4. SECOND COURSE RECIPES 84

CHAPTER 6.DESSERT RECIPES

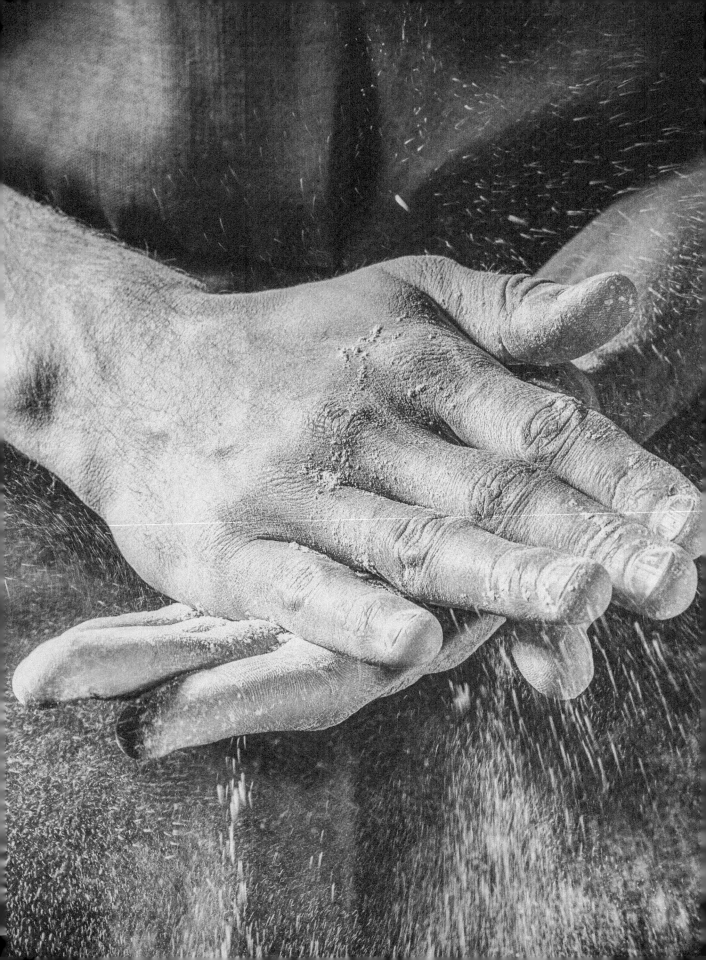

INTRODUCTION

*T*hose who have encountered diabetes in their lives learn first of all that diabetes is type 1 or type 2. In other words, insulin-dependent (IDDM) or non-insulin-dependent (NIDDM). The first is mainly sick in childhood or youth, and the second is more a companion of adulthood.

This distinction is essential for understanding what processes occur in the body and how to correct them. We remember that diabetes is called this because the body, at some point, stops absorbing sugar and leaves it drifting in the bloodstream. It complicates the functioning of internal organs, primarily the nervous tissue and the brain. Why is this happening?

In type 1 diabetes, the pancreas is the culprit. *More precisely, the part of it that is responsible for the production of insulin. Insulin is a hormone that, figuratively speaking, takes glucose molecules (this is the scientific name for sugar when it is absorbed from the stomach into the bloodstream) under the arms and "escorts" them into tissue cells. Without insulin, the cell remains closed, and glucose cannot get there with all the desire. It is bad both for the cell itself and for the organism as a whole. The cell, lacking glucose, loses its primary source of energy supply. All processes in it freeze, and the cell becomes unviable. It applies to all the cells that make up our muscles, bones, blood vessels, lining the walls of internal organs.*

But there are other issues in our body as well. Thus, the brain and nerve fibers cells can assimilate glucose without any "guides." They use it directly, regardless of whether the pancreas produces insulin or does not even smell in the body. Now let's see what happens in our body when we eat something sweet, but insulin is not produced. So, the stomach digests food and breaks down sugar into glucose. Glucose is taken up into the bloodstream through the stomach walls and travels through the internal organs. "Knock, Knock!" - and the muscle cells are closed. Simultaneously, they acutely feel the lack of energy and shout about this to the brain. The brain increases blood flow, pushing more glucose to the doors of cells, but cells, in the absence of insulin, simply "do not see" glucose and continue to signal energy deficiency. The body is once again spurred on, but no changes occur for the cells of these tissues. But where does the unclaimed glucose go? And with all its volume, it falls on the brain and nerve fibers cells, which are much less demanding concerning insulin. And they can be understood! Such a mechanism was conceived by nature so that when it is necessary to react faster in case of danger, additional energy will go to the brain and nerve fibers.

Alas, in the case of diabetes, nature's foresight turns against us. The fact is that all complications of diabetes are associated with just such a differentiated approach. When the cells of muscles and bone tissue close the doors to sugar - he has no choice but to seek refuge in more "pliable" cells. And the entire energy explosion falls on the brain and nervous system. That is why people with diabetes most often complain of confusion, pains of neurological origin, and their eyesight goes down.

To correct this imbalance, people with type 1 diabetes are forced to regularly take insulin preparations, injecting it into the body almost before every meal. But we also remember that there is non-insulin-dependent diabetes, the so-called type II diabetes. Even the name of the named variety of the disease implies that insulin has nothing to do with it. What happens in the body in this case?

In fact, in people with type 2 diabetes, the pancreas produces insulin regularly. But for some reason, the cells simply stop responding to it! Either they don't like the sight of it, or the smell - scientists have not figured it out yet. For us, the fact remains: no matter how much you add insulin to the body, the cells will not react to it. And then everything develops according to the scenario familiar to us - the internal organs scream about the lack of energy, the brain pumps up glucose, glucose provides an energy explosion, but not where it is needed, and further in a circle. The second type of diabetes therapy's main difference is that blood sugar is corrected here, not with artificial insulin, but with drugs that increase cell resistance. Simply put, substances

This is where the fun begins. It has long

been noted that with type 2 diabetes, the patient can generally refuse pills and injections - if he can choose a diet in which glucose will enter the bloodstream in strictly metered proportions and doses. The rest of the products will provide the body with an optimal existence. In type 1 diabetes, you can significantly reduce the number of insulin injections if you adhere to good nutrition principles. To understand what these principles are, we need to remember what we know about food in general.

CHAPTER 1. KNOW THE PROBLEM: THE DIET THAT CONTROLS BLOOD SUGAR

*D*eveloping diabetes later in life can be caused by a variety of things. One of these is being overweight. Eating many sugary foods and sweets does not cause diabetes, but it does lead to obesity and other health problems.

Having type 2 diabetes means that you have to monitor your food and balance your carbohydrates and sugars throughout the day. To help you out with that, let's look at some of the most frequently asked questions for other diabetics about sugar.

Do I need to eliminate sugar from my diet?

It is impossible to eliminate all sugar from any diet. Many foods contain sugar naturally, like fruit. Plus, our bodies

turn all carbohydrates into glucose for energy, a fancy word for blood sugar.

You can watch the amount of sugar you eat and make sure to avoid eating foods that have added sugar in them. When you look at the "total carbohydrates" on a label, know this number includes complex carbohydrates, sugar, and fiber. Monitoring carbohydrate intake is the best way for a person with diabetes to keep glucose within a normal range.

Which Foods Are High in Sugar?

You will be surprised to learn that many food items labeled "healthy" are relatively high in sugar. Here are 15 of the worst culprits that you should try to avoid or eat only occasionally:

1. Barbecue Sauce, a single serving,

about two tablespoons may have as many as three teaspoons of sugar.

2. Ketchup, like its cousin, BBQ sauce, it is full of sugar.

3. Fruit juice, you get more health benefits, and less sugar, by eating the actual fruit than drinking the juice.

4. Spaghetti Sauce, tomatoes naturally have some sugar in them, but many companies add sugar to their pasta sauces.

5. Sports Drinks are high in added sugars since they were designed for athletes who burn sugar quicker than the average human.

6. Chocolate Milk, while it delivers all the healthy nutrients of plain milk, also contains added sugar.

7. Granola, the oats used to make granola are full of fiber, carbs, and nutrients, but most granola contains over six teaspoons of sugar per 100 grams.

8. Flavored coffee, those tasty, trendy drinks can have up to 25 added teaspoons of sugar in every cup.

9. Iced Tea, if you buy your premade, it may have as much sugar as a can of soda.

10. Protein Bars, while eating protein can help you feel fuller longer and help with weight loss, most commercial protein bars are high in added sugar.

11. Like other "healthy" drinks, Vitamin water has added sugars; some may have as many as 32 grams per bottle.

12. Canned Soup, this one may surprise you, the vegetables used in the soup have natural sugars, but many companies add sugar to the soup.

13. Cereal Bars, just like sweetened breakfast cereals, have more sugar than you should eat in a day.

14. Canned or Processed Fruit, most canned fruit is packed in syrup, which adds more sugar; also, canned fruit loses most of its healthy fiber and nutrients during the processing.

15. Bottled Smoothies, mixing fruit and milk can provide many health benefits, but commercially made smoothies can have as many as 24 teaspoons of sugar in just one serving.

What Ingredients Should I Avoid?

Most processed food in the US is full of artificial chemicals, preservatives, and sugar. The easiest way to avoid them is to cook at home, this way you know what is in the food you eat. But when you have to buy something processed, read the label and avoid the following ingredients

- *High fructose corn syrup*

- *Dextrose*

- *Lactose*

- *Fructose*

- *Sucrose*

- *Malt syrup*

- *White granulated sugar*

- *Honey*

- *Agave nectar*

- *Maltodextrin*

- *Glucose*

How Much Sugar Can I Eat in a Day?

As you can see, completely avoiding sugar is just not possible. According to the American Heart Association, your sugar intake should be 10%, or less, of your daily calorie intake. For a diet of 1,200 calories per day, you should shoot for 120 – 100 grams of sugar or less.

You can increase your energy by eating foods high in fiber, lean proteins, and healthy fats. Also, eat smaller meals throughout the day, which will prevent the urge to snack on sugary foods and keep your blood sugar from spiking.

What are the Best Substitutes for Sugar?

Luckily, you will find plenty of sugar substitutes in the grocery store today. Sugar substitutes come in three primary varieties:

1. *Artificial sweeteners, these synthetic substitutes will not affect glucose levels, but they do tend to have an unpleasant aftertaste. Artificial sweeteners include saccharin, aspartame, sucralose, and neotame.*

2. *Sugar Alcohols, these occur naturally in some foods and are created to be added to others. Unlike artificial and natural sweeteners, these do have calories and can affect your glucose levels. Sugar alcohols include; sorbitol, lactitol, glycerol, and xylitol.*

3. *Natural sweeteners include honey, molasses, maple syrup, fruit juices, and nectars. You need to monitor the amount you use because they act just like sugar.*

However, a natural sweetener has no calories and will not cause a spike in glucose. Stevia is a sweetener extracted from Stevia rebaudiana. Substitutes made from the stevia plant include Splenda, Truvia, and Pur Via.

APPETIZER RECIPES

1. AROMATIC TOASTED PUMPKIN SEEDS

INGREDIENTS

- 1 cup pumpkin seeds
- 1 teaspoon cinnamon
- 2 packets stevia
- 1 tablespoon canola oil
- ¼ teaspoon sea salt

 **PREPARATION** 5 MIN

 **COOKING** 45 MIN

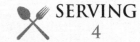 **SERVING** 4

DIRECTIONS

1. Prep the oven to 300°F (150°C).
2. Combine the pumpkin seeds with cinnamon, stevia, canola oil, and salt in a bowl. Stir to mix well.
3. Pour the seeds in the single layer on a baking sheet, then arrange the sheet in the preheated oven.
4. Bake for 45 minutes or until well toasted and fragrant. Shake the sheet twice to bake the seeds evenly.
5. Serve immediately.

Nutritions: *202 calories, 5.1g carbohydrates, 2.3g fiber*

2. BACON-WRAPPED SHRIMPS

INGREDIENTS

- 20 shrimps, peeled and deveined
- 7 slices bacon
- 4 leaves romaine lettuce

 **PREPARATION**
10 MIN

 **COOKING**
6 MIN

 **SERVING**
10

DIRECTIONS

1. Set the oven to 205°C.
2. Wrap each shrimp with each bacon strip, then arrange the wrapped shrimps in a single layer on a baking sheet, seam side down.
3. Broil for 6 minutes. Flip the shrimps halfway through the cooking time.
4. Take out from the oven and serve on lettuce leaves.

Nutritions: *70 calories, 4.5g fat, 7g protein*

3. CHEESY BROCCOLI BITES

INGREDIENTS

- 2 tablespoons olive oil
- 2 heads broccoli, trimmed
- 1 egg
- 1/3 cup reduced-fat shredded Cheddar cheese
- 1 egg white
- ½ cup onion, chopped
- 1/3 cup bread crumbs
- ¼ teaspoon salt
- ¼ teaspoon black pepper

 **PREPARATION** 10 MIN    **COOKING** 25 MIN   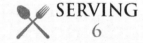 **SERVING** 6

DIRECTIONS

1. Ready the oven at 400°F (205°C). Coat a large baking sheet with olive oil.
2. Arrange a colander in a saucepan, then place the broccoli in the colander. Pour the water into the saucepan to cover the bottom. Boil, then reduce the heat to low. Close and simmer for 6 minutes. Allow cooling for 10 minutes.
3. Blend broccoli and remaining ingredients in a food processor. Let sit for 10 minutes.
4. Make the bites: Drop 1 tablespoon of the mixture on the baking sheet. Repeat with the remaining mixture.
5. Bake in the preheated oven for 25 minutes. Flip the bites halfway through the cooking time.
6. Serve immediately.

Nutritions: *100 calories, 13g carbohydrates, 3g fiber*

4. EASY CAPRESE SKEWERS

INGREDIENTS

- 12 cherry tomatoes
- 8 (1-inch) pieces Mozzarella cheese
- 12 basil leaves
- ¼ cup Italian Vinaigrette, for serving

 **PREPARATION**
5 MIN

 **COOKING**
0 MIN

 **SERVING**
2

DIRECTIONS

1. Thread the tomatoes, cheese, and bay leave alternatively through the skewers.
2. Place the skewers on a huge plate and baste with the Italian Vinaigrette. Serve immediately.

Nutritions: *230 calories, 8.5g carbohydrates, 1.9g fiber*

5. GRILLED TOFU WITH SESAME SEEDS

INGREDIENTS

- 1½ tablespoons brown rice vinegar
- 1 scallion
- 1 tablespoon ginger root
- 1 tablespoon no-sugar-added applesauce
- 2 tablespoons naturally brewed soy sauce
- ¼ teaspoon dried red pepper flakes
- 2 teaspoons sesame oil, toasted
- 1 (14-ounce / 397-g) package extra-

- firm tofu
- 2 tablespoons fresh cilantro
- 1 teaspoon sesame seeds

 **PREPARATION** 45 MIN

 **COOKING** 20 MIN

 **SERVING** 6

DIRECTIONS

1. Combine the vinegar, scallion, ginger, applesauce, soy sauce, red pepper flakes, and sesame oil in a large bowl. Stir to mix well.
2. Dunk the tofu pieces in the bowl, then refrigerate to marinate for 30 minutes.
3. Preheat a grill pan over medium-high heat.
4. Place the tofu on the grill pan with tongs, reserve the marinade, then grill for 8 minutes or until the tofu is golden brown and have deep grilled marks on both sides. Flip the tofu halfway through the cooking time.

You may need to work in batches to avoid overcrowding.
5. Transfer the tofu to a large plate and sprinkle with cilantro leaves and sesame seeds. Serve with the marinade alongside.

Nutritions: *90 calories, 3g carbohydrates, 1g fiber*

6. KALE CHIPS

INGREDIENTS

- ¼ teaspoon garlic powder
- Pinch cayenne to taste
- 1 tablespoon extra-virgin olive oil
- ½ teaspoon sea salt, or to taste
- 1 (8-ounce) bunch kale

 **PREPARATION**
5 MIN

 **COOKING**
15 MIN

 **SERVING**
1

DIRECTIONS

1. Prepare oven at 180°C. Line two baking sheets with parchment paper.
2. Toss the garlic powder, cayenne pepper, olive oil, and salt in a large bowl, then dunk the kale in the bowl.
3. Situate kale in a single layer on one of the baking sheets.
4. Arrange the sheet in the preheated oven and bake for 7 minutes. Remove the sheet from the oven and pour the kale into the single layer of the other baking sheet.
5. Move the sheet of kale back to the oven and bake for another 7 minutes.
6. Serve immediately.

Nutritions: *136 calories, 3g carbohydrates, 1.1g fiber*

7. SIMPLE DEVILED EGGS

INGREDIENTS

- 6 large eggs
- 1/8 teaspoon mustard powder
- 2 tablespoons light mayonnaise

 **PREPARATION**
5 MIN

 **COOKING**
8 MIN

 **SERVING**
12

DIRECTIONS

1. Sit the eggs in a saucepan, then pour in enough water to cover the egg. Bring to a boil, then boil the eggs for another 8 minutes. Turn off the heat and cover, then let sit for 15 minutes.
2. Transfer the boiled eggs to a pot of cold water and peel under the water.
3. Transfer the eggs to a large plate, then cut in half. Remove the egg yolks and place them in a bowl, then mash with a fork.
4. Add the mustard powder, mayo, salt, and pepper to the bowl of yolks, then stir to mix well.
5. Spoon the yolk mixture in the egg white on the plate. Serve immediately.

Nutritions: *45 calories, 1g carbohydrates, 0.9g fiber*

8. SAUTÉED COLLARD GREENS AND CABBAGE

INGREDIENTS

- 2 tablespoons extra-virgin olive oil
- 1 collard greens bunch
- ½ small green cabbage
- 6 garlic cloves
- 1 tablespoon low-sodium soy sauce

 **PREPARATION** 10 MIN

 **COOKING** 10 MIN

 **SERVING** 8

DIRECTIONS

1. Cook olive oil in a large skillet over medium-high heat.
2. Sauté the collard greens in the oil for about 2 minutes, or until the greens start to wilt.
3. Toss in the cabbage and mix well. Set to medium-low, cover, and cook for 5 to 7 minutes, stirring occasionally, or until the greens are softened.
4. Fold in the garlic and soy sauce and stir to combine. Cook for about 30 seconds more until fragrant.
5. Remove from the heat to a plate and serve.

Nutritions: *73 calories, 5.9g carbohydrates, 2.9g fiber*

9. ROASTED DELICATA SQUASH WITH THYME

INGREDIENTS

- 1 (1½-pound) Delicata squash
- 1 tablespoon extra-virgin olive oil
- ½ teaspoon dried thyme
- ¼ teaspoon salt
- ¼ teaspoon freshly ground black pepper

 **PREPARATION** 10 MIN  **COOKING** 20 MIN 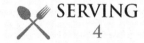 **SERVING** 4

DIRECTIONS

1. Prep the oven to 400°F (205°C). Ready baking sheet with parchment paper and set aside.
2. Add the squash strips, olive oil, thyme, salt, and pepper in a large bowl, and toss until the squash strips are fully coated.
3. Place the squash strips on the prepared baking sheet in a single layer. Roast for about 20 minutes, flipping the strips halfway through.
4. Remove from the oven and serve on plates.

Nutritions: *78 calories, 11.8g carbohydrates, 2.1g fiber*

10. ROASTED ASPARAGUS AND RED PEPPERS

INGREDIENTS

- 1-pound (454 g) asparagus
- 2 red bell peppers, seeded
- 1 small onion
- 2 tablespoons Italian dressing

 **PREPARATION**
5 MIN

 **COOKING**
15 MIN

 **SERVING**
4

DIRECTIONS

1. Ready oven to (205°C). Wrap baking sheet with parchment paper and set aside.
2. Combine the asparagus with the peppers, onion, dressing in a large bowl, and toss well.
3. Arrange the vegetables on the baking sheet and roast for about 15 minutes. Flip the vegetables with a spatula once during cooking.
4. Transfer to a large platter and serve.

Nutritions: *92 calories, 10.7g carbohydrates, 4g fiber*

11. TARRAGON SPRING PEAS

INGREDIENTS

- 1 tablespoon unsalted butter
- ½ Vidalia onion
- 1 cup low-sodium vegetable broth
- 3 cups fresh shelled peas
- 1 tablespoon minced fresh tarragon

 **PREPARATION**
10 MIN

 **COOKING**
12 MIN

 **SERVING**
6

DIRECTIONS

1. Cook butter in a pan at medium heat.
2. Sauté the onion in the melted butter for about 3 minutes, stirring occasionally.
3. Pour in the vegetable broth and whisk well. Add the peas and tarragon to the skillet and stir to combine.
4. Reduce the heat to low, cover, cook for about 8 minutes more, or until the peas are tender.
5. Let the peas cool for 5 minutes and serve warm.

Nutritions: *82 calories, 12g carbohydrates, 3.8g fiber*

12. BUTTER-ORANGE YAMS

INGREDIENTS

- 2 medium jewel yams
- 2 tablespoons unsalted butter
- Juice of 1 large orange
- 1½ teaspoons ground cinnamon
- ¼ teaspoon ground ginger
- ¾ teaspoon ground nutmeg
- 1/8 teaspoon ground cloves

 **PREPARATION**
7 MIN

 **COOKING**
45 MIN

 **SERVING**
8

DIRECTIONS

1. Set oven at 180°C.
2. Arrange the yam dices on a rimmed baking sheet in a single layer. Set aside.
3. Add the butter, orange juice, cinnamon, ginger, nutmeg, and garlic cloves to a medium saucepan over medium-low heat. Cook for 3 to 5 minutes, stirring continuously.
4. Spoon the sauce over the yams and toss to coat well.
5. Bake in the prepared oven for 40 minutes.
6. Let the yams cool for 8 minutes on the baking sheet before removing and serving.

Nutritions: *129 calories, 24.7g carbohydrates, 5g fiber*

13. ROASTED TOMATO BRUSSELS SPROUTS

INGREDIENTS

- 1-pound (454 g) Brussels sprouts
- 1 tablespoon extra-virgin olive oil
- ½ cup sun-dried tomatoes
- 2 tablespoons lemon juice
- 1 teaspoon lemon zest

 **PREPARATION** 15 MIN    **COOKING** 20 MIN   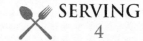 **SERVING** 4

DIRECTIONS

1. Set oven 205°C. Prep large baking sheet with aluminum foil.
2. Toss the Brussels sprouts in the olive oil in a large bowl until well coated. Sprinkle with salt and pepper.
3. Spread out the seasoned Brussels sprouts on the prepared baking sheet in a single layer.
4. Roast for 20 minutes, shake halfway through.
5. Remove from the oven then situate in a bowl. Whisk tomatoes, lemon juice, and lemon zest, to incorporate. Serve immediately.

Nutritions: *111 calories, 13.7g carbohydrates, 4.9g fiber*

14. SIMPLE SAUTÉED GREENS

INGREDIENTS

- 2 tablespoons extra-virgin olive oil
- 1 pound (454 g) Swiss chard
- 1-pound (454 g) kale
- ½ teaspoon ground cardamom
- 1 tablespoon lemon juice

 **PREPARATION** 10 MIN  **COOKING** 10 MIN  **SERVING** 4

DIRECTIONS

1. Heat up olive oil in a big skillet over medium-high heat.
2. Stir in Swiss chard, kale, cardamom, lemon juice to the skillet, and stir to combine. Cook for about 10 minutes, stirring continuously, or until the greens are wilted.
3. Sprinkle with the salt and pepper and stir well.
4. Serve the greens on a plate while warm.

Nutritions: *139 calories, 15.8g carbohydrates, 3.9g fiber*

15. GARLICKY MUSHROOMS

INGREDIENTS

- 1 tablespoon butter
- 2 teaspoons extra-virgin olive oil
- 2 pounds button mushrooms
- 2 teaspoons minced fresh garlic
- 1 teaspoon chopped fresh thyme

 **PREPARATION**
10 MIN

 **COOKING**
12 MIN

 **SERVING**
4

DIRECTIONS

1. Warm up butter and olive oil in a huge skillet over medium-high heat.
2. Add the mushrooms and sauté for 10 minutes, stirring occasionally.
3. Stir in the garlic and thyme and cook for an additional 2 minutes.
4. Season and serve on a plate.

Nutritions: *96 calories, 8.2g carbohydrates, 1.7g fiber*

16. GREEN BEANS IN OVEN

INGREDIENTS

- 12 oz. green bean pods
- 1 tbsp. olive oil
- 1/2 tsp. onion powder
- 1/8 tsp. pepper
- 1/8 tsp. salt

 **PREPARATION**
15 MIN

 **COOKING**
17 MIN

 **SERVING**
3

DIRECTIONS

1. Preheat oven to 350°F. Mix green beans with onion powder, pepper, and oil.
2. Spread the seeds on the baking sheet.
3. Bake 17 minutes or until you have a delicious aroma in the kitchen.

Nutritions: *37 Calories, 1.4g Protein, 5.5g Carbohydrates*

17. PARMESAN BROILED FLOUNDER

INGREDIENTS

- 2 (4-oz) flounder
- 1,5 tbsp Parmesan cheese
- 1,5 tbsp mayonnaise
- 1/8 tsp soy sauce
- 1/4 tsp chili sauce
- 1/8 tsp salt-free lemon-pepper seasoning

 **PREPARATION**
10 MIN

 **COOKING**
7 MIN

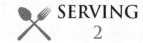 **SERVING**
2

DIRECTIONS

1. Preheat flounder.
2. Mix cheese, reduced-fat mayonnaise, soy sauce, chili sauce, seasoning.
3. Put fish on a baking sheet coated with cooking spray, sprinkle with salt and pepper.
4. Spread Parmesan mixture over flounder.
5. Broil 6 to 8 minutes or until a crust appears on the fish.

Nutritions: 200 Calories, 17g Fat, 7g Carbohydrate

18. FISH WITH FRESH TOMATO - BASIL SAUCE

INGREDIENTS

- 2 (4-oz) tilapia fillets
- 1 tbsp fresh basil, chopped
- 1/8 tsp salt
- 1 pinch of crushed red pepper
- 1 cup cherry tomatoes, chopped
- 2 tsp extra virgin olive oil

 **PREPARATION** 10 MIN

 **COOKING** 15 MIN

 **SERVING** 2

DIRECTIONS

1. Preheat oven to 400°F.
2. Arrange rinsed and patted dry fish fillets on foil (coat a foil baking sheet with cooking spray).
3. Sprinkle tilapia fillets with salt and red pepper.
4. Bake 12 - 15 minutes.
5. Meanwhile, mix leftover ingredients in a saucepan.
6. Cook over medium-high heat until tomatoes are tender.
7. Top fish fillets properly with tomato mixture.

Nutritions: *130 Calories, 30g Protein, 1g Carbohydrates*

19. BAKED CHICKEN

INGREDIENTS

- 2 (6-oz) bone-in chicken breasts
- 1/8 tsp salt
- 1/8 tsp pepper
- 3 tsp extra virgin olive oil
- 1/2 tsp dried oregano
- 7 pitted kalamata olives
- 1 cup cherry tomatoes
- 1/2 cup onion
- 1 (9-oz) pkg frozen artichoke hearts
- 1 lemon

 **PREPARATION** 15 MIN  **COOKING** 25 MIN 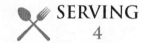 **SERVING** 4

DIRECTIONS

1. Preheat oven to 400°F.
2. Sprinkle chicken with pepper, salt, and oregano.
3. Heat oil, add chicken and cook until it browned.
4. Place chicken in a baking dish. Arrange tomatoes, coarsely chopped olives, and onion, artichokes and lemon cut into wedges around the chicken.
5. Bake 20 minutes or until chicken is done and vegetables are tender.

Nutritions: *160 Calories, 3g Fat, 1g Carbohydrates*

20. SEARED CHICKEN WITH ROASTED VEGETABLES

INGREDIENTS

- 1 (8-oz) boneless, skinless chicken breasts
- 3/4 lb. small Brussels sprouts
- 2 large carrots
- 1 large red bell pepper
- 1 small red onion
- 2 cloves garlic halved
- 2 tbsp extra virgin olive oil
- 1/2 tsp dried dill
- 1/4 tsp pepper
- 1/4 tsp salt

 **PREPARATION**
20 MIN

 **COOKING**
30 MIN

 **SERVING**
1

DIRECTIONS

1. 1.Preheat oven to 425°F.
2. Match Brussels sprouts cut in half, red onion cut into wedges, sliced carrots, bell pepper cut into pieces and halved garlic on a baking sheet.
3. Sprinkle with 1 tbsp oil and with 1/8 tsp salt and 1/8 tsp pepper. Bake until well-roasted, cool slightly.
4. In the Meantime, sprinkle chicken with dill, remaining 1/8 tsp salt and 1/8 tsp pepper. Cook until chicken is done. Put roasted vegetables with drippings over chicken.

Nutritions: *170 Calories, 7g Fat, 12g Protein*

21. FISH SIMMERED IN TOMATO-PEPPER SAUCE

INGREDIENTS

- 2 (4-oz) cod fillets
- 1 big tomato
- 1/3 cup red peppers (roasted)
- 3 tbsp almonds
- 2 cloves garlic
- 2 tbsp fresh basil leaves
- 2 tbsp extra virgin olive oil
- 1/4 tsp salt
- 1/8 tsp pepper

 **PREPARATION** 5 MIN

 **COOKING** 10 MIN

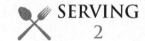 **SERVING** 2

DIRECTIONS

1. Toast sliced almonds in a pan until fragrant.
2. Grind almonds, basil, minced garlic, 1-2 tsp oil in a food processor until finely ground.
3. Add coarsely-chopped tomato and red peppers; grind until smooth.
4. Season fish with salt and pepper.
5. Cook in hot oil in a large pan over medium-high heat until fish is browned. Pour sauce around fish. Cook 6 minutes more.

Nutritions: *90 Calories, 5g Fat, 7g Carbohydrates*

22. CHEESE POTATO AND PEA CASSEROLE

INGREDIENTS

- 1 tbsp olive oil
- ¾ lb. red potatoes
- ¾ cup green peas
- ½ cup red onion
- ¼ tsp dried rosemary
- ¼ tsp salt
- 1/8 tsp pepper

 **PREPARATION**
10 MIN

 **COOKING**
35 MIN

 **SERVING**
3

DIRECTIONS

1. Prepare oven to 350°F.
2. Cook 1 tsp oil in a skillet. Stir in thinly sliced onions and cook. Remove from pan.
3. Situate half of the thinly sliced potatoes and onions in bottom of skillet; top with peas, crushed dried rosemary, and 1/8 tsp each salt and pepper.
4. Place remaining potatoes and onions on top. Season with remaining 1/8 tsp salt.
5. Bake 35 minutes, pour remaining 2 tsp oil and sprinkle with cheese.

Nutritions: *80 Calories, 2g Protein, 18g Carbohydrates*

23. OVEN-FRIED TILAPIA

INGREDIENTS

- 2 (4-oz) tilapia fillets
- 1/4 cup yellow cornmeal
- 2 tbsp light ranch dressing
- 1 tbsp canola oil
- 1 tsp dill (dried)
- 1/8 tsp salt

 **PREPARATION**
7 MIN

 **COOKING**
15 MIN

 **SERVING**
2

DIRECTIONS

1. Preheat oven to 425°F. Brush both sides of rinsed and patted dry tilapia fish fillets with dressing.
2. Combine cornmeal, oil, dill, and salt.
3. Sprinkle fish fillets with cornmeal mixture.
4. Put fish on a prepared baking sheet.
5. Bake 15 minutes.

Nutritions: *96 Calories, 21g Protein, 2g Fat*

24. CHICKEN WITH COCONUT SAUCE

INGREDIENTS

- 1/2 lb. chicken breasts
- 1/3 cup red onion
- 1 tbsp paprika (smoked)
- 2 tsp cornstarch
- 1/2 cup light coconut milk
- 1 tsp extra virgin olive oil
- 2 tbsp fresh cilantro
- 1 (10-oz) can tomatoes and green chilis
- 1/4 cup water

 **PREPARATION** 15 MIN    **COOKING** 20 MIN    **SERVING** 2

DIRECTIONS

1. Cut chicken into little cubes; sprinkle with 1,5 tsp paprika.
2. Heat oil, add chicken and cook 3 to 5 minutes.
3. Remove from skillet, and fry finely-chopped onion 5 minutes.
4. Return chicken to pan. Add tomatoes,1,5 tsp paprika, and water. Bring to a boil, and then simmer 4 minutes.
5. Mix cornstarch and coconut milk; stir into chicken mixture, and cook until it has done.
6. Sprinkle with chopped cilantro.

Nutritions: *200 Calories, 13g Protein, 10g Fat*

25. FISH WITH FRESH HERB SAUCE

INGREDIENTS

- 2 (4-oz) cod fillets
- 1/3 cup fresh cilantro
- 1/4 tsp cumin
- 1 tbsp red onion
- 2 tsp extra virgin olive oil
- 1 tsp red wine vinegar
- 1 small clove garlic
- 1/8 tsp salt
- 1/8 black pepper

 **PREPARATION**
10 MIN

 **COOKING**
10 MIN

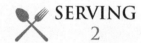 **SERVING**
2

DIRECTIONS

1. Combine chopped cilantro, finely chopped onion, oil, red wine vinegar, minced garlic, and salt.
2. Sprinkle both sides of fish fillets with cumin and pepper.
3. Cook fillets 4 minutes per side. Top each fillet with cilantro mixture.

Nutritions: *90 Calories, 4g Fat, 3g Carbohydrates*

26. SKILLET TURKEY PATTIES

INGREDIENTS

- 1/2 lb. lean ground turkey
- 1/2 cup low-sodium chicken broth
- 1/4 cup red onion
- 1/2 tsp Worcestershire sauce
- 1 tsp extra virgin olive oil
- 1/4 tsp oregano (dried)
- 1/8 tsp pepper

 **PREPARATION**
7 MIN

 **COOKING**
8 MIN

 **SERVING**
2

DIRECTIONS

1. Combine turkey, chopped onion, Worcestershire sauce, dried oregano, and pepper; make 2 patties.
2. Warm up oil and cook patties 4 minutes per side; set aside.
3. Add broth to skillet, bring to a boil. Boil 2 minutes, spoon sauce over patties.

Nutritions: *180 Calories, 11g Fat, 9g Carbohydrates*

27. TURKEY LOAF

INGREDIENTS

- 1/2 lb. 93% lean ground turkey
- 1/3 cup panko breadcrumbs
- 1/2 cup green onion
- 1 egg
- 1/2 cup green bell pepper
- 1 tbsp ketchup
- 1/4 cup sauce (Picante)
- 1/2 tsp cumin (ground)

 **PREPARATION**
10 MIN

 **COOKING**
50 MIN

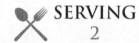 **SERVING**
2

DIRECTIONS

1. Preheat oven to 350°F. Mix lean ground turkey, 3 tbsp Picante sauce, panko breadcrumbs, egg, chopped green onion, chopped green bell pepper and cumin in a bowl (mix well);
2. Put the mixture into a baking sheet; shape into an oval (about 1,5 inches thick). Bake 45 minutes.
3. Mix remaining Picante sauce and the ketchup; apply over loaf. Bake 5 minutes longer. Let stand 5 minutes.

Nutritions: *161 Calories, 20g Protein, 8g Fat*

28. MUSHROOM PASTA

INGREDIENTS

- 4 oz whole-grain linguine
- 1 tsp extra virgin olive oil
- 1/2 cup light sauce
- 2 tbsp green onion
- 1 (8-oz) pkg mushrooms
- 1 clove garlic
- 1/8 tsp salt
- 1/8 tsp pepper

 **PREPARATION** 7MIN  **COOKING** 10 MIN  **SERVING** 4

DIRECTIONS

1. Cook pasta according to package directions, drain.
2. Fry sliced mushrooms 4 minutes.
3. Stir in fettuccine minced garlic, salt and pepper. Cook 2 minutes.
4. Heat light sauce until heated; top pasta mixture properly with sauce and with finely-chopped green onion.

Nutritions: *300 Calories, 1g Fat, 15g Carbohydrates*

29. CHICKEN TIKKA MASALA

INGREDIENTS

- 1/2 lb. chicken breasts
- 1/4 cup onion
- 1.5 tsp extra virgin olive oil
- 1 (14.5-oz) can tomatoes
- 1 tsp ginger
- 1 tsp fresh lemon juice
- 1/3 cup plain Greek yogurt (fat-free)
- 1 tbsp garam masala
- 1/4 tsp salt
- 1/4 tsp pepper

 **PREPARATION** 5 MIN    **COOKING** 15 MIN   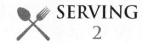 **SERVING** 2

DIRECTIONS

1. Flavor chicken cut into 1-inch cubes with 1,5 tsp garam masala,1/8 tsp salt and pepper.
2. Cook chicken and diced onion 4 to 5 minutes.
3. Add diced tomatoes, grated ginger, 1.5 tsp garam masala, 1/8 tsp salt. Cook 8 to 10 minutes.
4. Add lemon juice and yogurt until blended.

Nutritions: *200 Calories, 26g Protein, 10g Fat*

30. TOMATO AND ROASTED COD

INGREDIENTS

- 2 (4-oz) cod fillets
- 1 cup cherry tomatoes
- 2/3 cup onion
- 2 tsp orange rind
- 1 tbsp extra virgin olive oil
- 1 tsp thyme (dried)
- 1/4 tsp salt, divided
- 1/4 tsp pepper, divided

 **PREPARATION** 10 MIN    **COOKING** 35 MIN    **SERVING** 2

DIRECTIONS

1. Preheat oven to 400°F. Mix in half tomatoes, sliced onion, grated orange rind, extra virgin olive oil, dried thyme, and 1/8 salt and pepper. Fry 25 minutes. Remove from oven.
2. Arrange fish on pan, and flavor with remaining 1/8 tsp each salt and pepper. Put reserved tomato mixture over fish. Bake 10 minutes.

Nutritions: *120 Calories, 9g Protein, 2g Fat*

CHAPTER 3. FIRST COURSE RECIPES

31. GAZPACHO

INGREDIENTS

- 3 pounds ripe tomatoes
- 1 cup low-sodium tomato juice
- ½ red onion, chopped
- 1 cucumber
- 1 red bell pepper
- 2 celery stalks
- 2 tablespoons parsley
- 2 garlic cloves
- 2 tablespoons extra-virgin olive oil
- 2 tablespoons red wine vinegar
- 1 teaspoon honey
- ½ teaspoon salt
- ¼ teaspoon freshly ground black pepper

 **PREPARATION**
15 MIN

 **COOKING**
0 MIN

 **SERVING**
4

DIRECTIONS

1. In a blender jar, combine the tomatoes, tomato juice, onion, cucumber, bell pepper, celery, parsley, garlic, olive oil, vinegar, honey, salt, and pepper. Pulse until blended but still slightly chunky.
2. Adjust the seasonings as needed and serve.

Nutritions: *170 Calories, 24g Carbohydrates, 16g Sugars*

32. TOMATO AND KALE SOUP

INGREDIENTS

- 1 tablespoon extra-virgin olive oil
- 1 medium onion
- 2 carrots
- 3 garlic cloves
- 4 cups low-sodium vegetable broth
- 1 (28-ounce) can crushed tomatoes
- ½ teaspoon dried oregano
- ¼ teaspoon dried basil
- 4 cups chopped baby kale leaves
- ¼ teaspoon salt

 **PREPARATION** 10 MIN    **COOKING** 15 MIN    **SERVING** 4

DIRECTIONS

1. In a huge pot, heat up oil over medium heat. Sauté onion and carrots for 3 to 5 minutes. Add the garlic and sauté for 30 seconds more, until fragrant.
2. Add the vegetable broth, tomatoes, oregano, and basil to the pot and boil. Decrease the heat to low and simmer for 5 minutes.
3. Using an immersion blender, purée the soup.
4. Add the kale and simmer for 3 more minutes. Season with the salt. Serve immediately.

Nutritions: *170 Calories, 31g Carbohydrates, 13g Sugars*

33. COMFORTING SUMMER SQUASH SOUP WITH CRISPY CHICKPEAS

INGREDIENTS

- 1 (15-ounce) can low-sodium chickpeas
- 1 teaspoon extra-virgin olive oil
- ¼ teaspoon smoked paprika
- Pinch salt, plus ½ teaspoon
- 3 medium zucchinis
- 3 cups low-sodium vegetable broth
- ½ onion
- 3 garlic cloves
- 2 tablespoons plain low-fat Greek yogurt
- Freshly ground black pepper

 **PREPARATION** 10 MIN

 **COOKING** 20 MIN

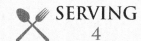 **SERVING** 4

DIRECTIONS

1. Preheat the oven to 425°F. Line a baking sheet with parchment paper.
2. In a medium mixing bowl, toss the chickpeas with 1 teaspoon of olive oil, the smoked paprika, and a pinch salt. Transfer to the prepared baking sheet and roast until crispy, about 20 minutes, stirring once. Set aside.
3. Meanwhile, in a medium pot, heat the remaining 1 tablespoon of oil over medium heat.
4. Add the zucchini, broth, onion, and garlic to the pot, and boil. Simmer, and cook for 20 minutes.
5. In a blender jar, purée the soup.

Return to the pot.
6. Add the yogurt, remaining ½ teaspoon of salt, and pepper, and stir well. Serve topped with the roasted chickpeas.

Nutritions: *188 Calories, 24g Carbohydrates, 7g Sugars*

34. CURRIED CARROT SOUP

INGREDIENTS

- 1 tablespoon extra-virgin olive oil
- 1 small onion
- 2 celery stalks
- 1½ teaspoons curry powder
- 1 teaspoon ground cumin
- 1 teaspoon minced fresh ginger
- 6 medium carrots
- 4 cups low-sodium vegetable broth
- ¼ teaspoon salt
- 1 cup canned coconut milk
- ¼ teaspoon freshly ground black pepper
- 1 tablespoon chopped fresh cilantro

 **PREPARATION** 10 MIN

 **COOKING** 5 MIN

 **SERVING** 6

DIRECTIONS

1. Heat an Instant Pot to high and add the olive oil.
2. Sauté the onion and celery for 2 to 3 minutes. Add the curry powder, cumin, and ginger to the pot and cook until fragrant, about 30 seconds.
3. Add the carrots, vegetable broth, and salt to the pot. Close and seal, and set for 5 minutes on high. Allow the pressure to release naturally.
4. In a blender jar, carefully purée the soup in batches and transfer back to the pot.
5. Stir in the coconut milk and pepper, and heat through. Top with the cilantro and serve.

Nutritions: *145 Calories, 13g Carbohydrates, 4g Sugars*

35. THAI PEANUT, CARROT, AND SHRIMP SOUP

INGREDIENTS

- 1 tablespoon coconut oil
- 1 tablespoon Thai red curry paste
- ½ onion
- 3 garlic cloves
- 2 cups chopped carrots
- ½ cup whole unsalted peanuts
- 4 cups low-sodium vegetable broth
- ½ cup unsweetened plain almond milk
- ½ pound shrimp,

- Minced fresh cilantro, for garnish

 **PREPARATION** 10 MIN

 **COOKING** 10 MIN

 **SERVING** 4

DIRECTIONS

1. In a big pan, heat up oil over medium-high heat until shimmering.
2. Cook curry paste, stirring continuously, for 1 minute. Add the onion, garlic, carrots, and peanuts to the pan, and continue to cook for 2 to 3 minutes.
3. Boil broth. Reduce the heat to low and simmer for 5 to 6 minutes.
4. Purée the soup until smooth and return it to the pot. Over low heat, pour almond milk and stir to combine. Cook shrimp in the pot for 2 to 3 minutes.
5. Garnish with cilantro and serve.

Nutritions: 237 Calories, 17g Carbohydrates, 6g Sugars

36. CHICKEN TORTILLA SOUP

INGREDIENTS

- 1 tablespoon extra-virgin olive oil
- 1 onion, thinly sliced
- 1 garlic clove, minced
- 1 jalapeño pepper, diced
- 2 boneless, skinless chicken breasts
- 4 cups low-sodium chicken broth
- 1 roma tomato, diced
- ½ teaspoon salt
- 2 (6-inch) corn tortillas
- Juice of 1 lime
- Minced fresh cilantro, for garnish
- ¼ cup shredded cheddar cheese, for garnish

 **PREPARATION** 10 MIN

 **COOKING** 35 MIN

 **SERVING** 4

DIRECTIONS

1. In a medium pot, cook oil over medium-high heat. Add the onion and cook for 3 to 5 minutes until it begins to soften. Add the garlic and jalapeño, and cook until fragrant, about 1 minute more.
2. Add the chicken, chicken broth, tomato, and salt to the pot and boil. Lower heat to medium and simmer mildly for 20 to 25 minutes. Remove the chicken from the pot and set aside.
3. Preheat a broiler to high.
4. Spray the tortilla strips with nonstick cooking spray and toss to coat. Spread in a single layer on a baking sheet and broil for 3 to 5 minutes, flipping once, until crisp.
5. Once chicken is cooked, shred it with two forks and return to the pot.
6. Season the soup with the lime juice. Serve hot, garnished with cilantro, cheese, and tortilla strips.

Nutritions: *191 Calories, 13g Carbohydrates, 2g Sugars*

37. BEEF AND MUSHROOM BARLEY SOUP

INGREDIENTS

- 1-pound beef stew meat, cubed
- ¼ teaspoon salt
- ¼ teaspoon freshly ground black pepper
- 1 tablespoon extra-virgin olive oil
- 8 ounces sliced mushrooms
- 1 onion, chopped
- 2 carrots, chopped
- 3 celery stalks, chopped
- 6 garlic cloves, minced
- ½ teaspoon dried thyme
- 4 cups low-sodium beef broth
- 1 cup water
- ½ cup pearl barley

 **PREPARATION** 10 MIN

 **COOKING** 80 MIN

 **SERVING** 6

DIRECTIONS

1. Season the meat well.
2. In an Instant Pot, heat the oil over high heat. Cook meat on all sides. Remove from the pot and set aside.
3. Add the mushrooms to the pot and cook for 1 to 2 minutes. Remove the mushrooms and set aside with the meat.
4. Sauté onion, carrots, and celery for 3 to 4 minutes. Add the garlic and continue to cook until fragrant, about 30 seconds longer.
5. Return the meat and mushrooms to the pot, then add the thyme, beef broth, and water. Adjust the pressure on high and cook for 15 minutes. Let the pressure release naturally.
6. Open the Instant Pot and add the barley. Use the slow cooker function on the Instant Pot, affix the lid (vent open), and continue to cook for 1 hour. Serve.

Nutritions: *245 Calories, 19g Carbohydrates, 3g Sugars*

38. CUCUMBER, TOMATO, AND AVOCADO SALAD

INGREDIENTS

- 1 cup cherry tomatoes
- 1 large cucumber
- 1 small red onion
- 1 avocado
- 2 tablespoons chopped fresh dill
- 2 tablespoons extra-virgin olive oil
- Juice of 1 lemon
- ¼ teaspoon salt
- ¼ teaspoon freshly ground black pepper

 **PREPARATION** 10 MIN    **COOKING** 0 MIN    **SERVING** 4

DIRECTIONS

1. In a big mixing bowl, mix the tomatoes, cucumber, onion, avocado, and dill.
2. In a small bowl, combine the oil, lemon juice, salt, and pepper, and mix well.
3. Drizzle the dressing over the vegetables and toss to combine. Serve.

Nutritions: *151 Calories, 11g Carbohydrates, 4g Sugars*

39. CABBAGE SLAW SALAD

INGREDIENTS

- 2 cups green cabbage
- 2 cups red cabbage
- 2 cups grated carrots
- 3 scallions
- 2 tablespoons extra-virgin olive oil
- 2 tablespoons rice vinegar
- 1 teaspoon honey
- 1 garlic clove
- ¼ teaspoon salt

 **PREPARATION**
15 MIN

 **COOKING**
0 MIN

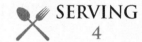 **SERVING**
4

DIRECTIONS

1. Throw together the green and red cabbage, carrots, and scallions.
2. In a small bowl, whisk together the oil, vinegar, honey, garlic, and salt.
3. Pour the dressing over the veggies and mix to combine thoroughly.
4. Serve immediately, or cover and chill for several hours before serving.

Nutritions: *80 Calories, 10g Carbohydrates, 6g Sugars*

40. GREEN SALAD WITH BLACKBERRIES, GOAT CHEESE, AND SWEET POTATOES

INGREDIENTS

For the vinaigrette
- 1-pint blackberries
- 2 tablespoons red wine vinegar
- 1 tablespoon honey
- 3 tablespoons extra-virgin olive oil
- ¼ teaspoon salt
- Freshly ground black pepper

For the salad
- 1 sweet potato, cubed
- 1 teaspoon extra-virgin olive oil
- 8 cups salad greens (baby spinach, spicy greens, romaine)
- ½ red onion, sliced
- ¼ cup crumbled goat cheese

 **PREPARATION** 15 MIN

 **COOKING** 20 MIN

 **SERVING** 4

DIRECTIONS

For vinaigrette
1. In a blender jar, combine the blackberries, vinegar, honey, oil, salt, and pepper, and process until smooth. Set aside.

For salad
2. Preheat the oven to 425°F. Line a baking sheet with parchment paper.
3. Mix the sweet potato with the olive oil. Transfer to the prepared baking sheet and roast for 20 minutes, stirring once halfway through, until tender. Remove and cool for a few minutes.

4. In a large bowl, toss the greens with the red onion and cooled sweet potato, and drizzle with the vinaigrette. Serve topped with 1 tablespoon of goat cheese per serving.

Nutritions: *196 Calories, 21g Carbohydrates, 10g Sugars*

41. THREE BEAN AND BASIL SALAD

INGREDIENTS

- 1 (15-ounce) can low-sodium chickpeas
- 1 (15-ounce) can low-sodium kidney beans
- 1 (15-ounce) can low-sodium white beans
- 1 red bell pepper
- ¼ cup chopped scallions
- ¼ cup finely chopped fresh basil
- 3 garlic cloves, minced
- 2 tablespoons extra-virgin olive oil
- 1 tablespoon red wine vinegar
- 1 teaspoon Dijon mustard
- ¼ teaspoon freshly ground black pepper

 **PREPARATION** 15 MIN

 **COOKING** 0 MIN

 **SERVING** 8

DIRECTIONS

1. Toss chickpeas, kidney beans, white beans, bell pepper, scallions, basil, and garlic gently.
2. Blend together olive oil, vinegar, mustard, and pepper. Toss with the salad.
3. Wrap and chill for 1 hour.

Nutritions: *193 Calories, 29g Carbohydrates, 3g Sugars*

42. RAINBOW BLACK BEAN SALAD

INGREDIENTS

- 1 (15-ounce) can low-sodium black beans
- 1 avocado, diced
- 1 cup cherry tomatoes, halved
- 1 cup chopped baby spinach
- ½ cup red bell pepper
- ¼ cup jicama
- ½ cup scallions
- ¼ cup fresh cilantro

- 2 tablespoons lime juice
- 1 tablespoon extra-virgin olive oil
- 2 garlic cloves, minced
- 1 teaspoon honey
- ¼ teaspoon salt
- ¼ teaspoon freshly ground black pepper

 **PREPARATION** 10 MIN

 **COOKING** 0 MIN

 **SERVING** 5

DIRECTIONS

1. Mix black beans, avocado, tomatoes, spinach, bell pepper, jicama, scallions, and cilantro.
2. Blend lime juice, oil, garlic, honey, salt, and pepper. Add to the salad and toss.
3. Chill for 1 hour before serving.

Nutritions: *169 Calories, 22g Carbohydrates, 3g Sugars*

43. WARM BARLEY AND SQUASH SALAD

INGREDIENTS

- 1 small butternut squash
- 3 tablespoons extra-virgin olive oil
- 2 cups broccoli florets
- 1 cup pearl barley
- 1 cup toasted chopped walnuts
- 2 cups baby kale
- ½ red onion, sliced
- 2 tablespoons balsamic vinegar
- 2 garlic cloves, minced
- ½ teaspoon salt
- ¼ teaspoon black pepper

 **PREPARATION** 20 MIN

 **COOKING** 0 MIN

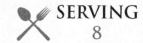 **SERVING** 8

DIRECTIONS

1. Preheat the oven to 400°F. Line a baking sheet with parchment paper.
2. Peel off the squash, and slice into dice. In a large bowl, toss the squash with 2 teaspoons of olive oil. Transfer to the prepared baking sheet and roast for 20 minutes.
3. While the squash is roasting, toss the broccoli in the same bowl with 1 teaspoon of olive oil. After 20 minutes, flip the squash and push it to one side of the baking sheet. Add the broccoli to the other side and continue to roast for 20 more minutes until tender.
4. While the veggies are roasting, in a medium pot, cover the barley with several inches of water. Boil, then adjust heat, cover, and simmer for 30 minutes until tender. Drain and rinse.
5. Transfer the barley to a large bowl, and toss with the cooked squash and broccoli, walnuts, kale, and onion.
6. In a small bowl, mix the remaining 2 tablespoons of olive oil, balsamic vinegar, garlic, salt, and pepper. Drizzle dressing over the salad and toss.

Nutritions: *274 Calories, 32g Carbohydrates, 3g Sugars*

44. WINTER CHICKEN AND CITRUS SALAD

INGREDIENTS

- 4 cups baby spinach
- 2 tablespoons extra-virgin olive oil
- 1 tablespoon lemon juice
- 1/8 teaspoon salt
- 2 cups chopped cooked chicken
- 2 mandarin oranges
- ½ peeled grapefruit, sectioned
- ¼ cup sliced almonds

 **PREPARATION** 10 MIN  **COOKING** 0 MIN  **SERVING** 4

DIRECTIONS

1. Toss spinach with the olive oil, lemon juice, salt, and pepper.
2. Add the chicken, oranges, grapefruit, and almonds to the bowl. Toss gently.
3. Arrange on 4 plates and serve.

Nutritions: *249 Calories, 11g Carbohydrates, 7g Sugars*

45. BLUEBERRY AND CHICKEN SALAD

INGREDIENTS

- 2 cups chopped cooked chicken
- 1 cup fresh blueberries
- ¼ cup almonds
- 1 celery stalk
- ¼ cup red onion
- 1 tablespoon fresh basil
- 1 tablespoon fresh cilantro
- ½ cup plain, vegan mayonnaise
- ¼ teaspoon salt
- ¼ teaspoon freshly ground black

- pepper
- 8 cups salad greens

 **PREPARATION** 10 MIN

 **COOKING** 0 MIN

 **SERVING** 4

DIRECTIONS

1. Toss chicken, blueberries, almonds, celery, onion, basil, and cilantro.
2. Blend yogurt, salt, and pepper. Stir chicken salad to combine.
3. Situate 2 cups of salad greens on each of 4 plates and divide the chicken salad among the plates to serve.

Nutritions: *207 Calories, 11g Carbohydrates, 6g Sugars*

46. BEEF AND RED BEAN CHILI

INGREDIENTS

- 1 cup dry red beans
- 1 tablespoon olive oil
- 2 pounds boneless beef chuck
- 1 large onion, coarsely chopped
- 1 (14 ounce) can beef broth
- 2 chipotle chili peppers in adobo sauce
- 2 teaspoons dried oregano, crushed
- 1 teaspoon ground cumin
- ½ teaspoon salt
- 1 (14.5 ounce) can tomatoes with mild green chilis
- 1 (15 ounce) can tomato sauce
- ¼ cup snipped fresh cilantro
- 1 medium red sweet pepper

 **PREPARATION** 10 MIN

 **COOKING** 6 H

 **SERVING** 4

DIRECTIONS

1. Rinse out the beans and place them into a Dutch oven or big saucepan, then add in water enough to cover them. Allow the beans to boil then drop the heat down. Simmer the beans without a cover for 10 minutes. Take off the heat and keep covered for an hour.
2. In a big frypan, heat up the oil upon medium-high heat, then cook onion and half the beef until they brown a bit over medium-high heat. Move into a 3 1/2- or 4-quart crockery cooker. Do this again with what's left of the beef. Add in tomato sauce, tomatoes (not drained), salt, cumin, oregano, adobo sauce, chipotle peppers, and broth, stirring to blend. Strain out and rinse beans and stir in the cooker.
3. Cook while covered on a low setting for around 10-12 hours or on high setting for 5-6 hours. Spoon the chili into bowls or mugs and top with sweet pepper and cilantro.

Nutritions: *288 Calories, 24g Carbohydrate, 5g Sugar*

47. BERRY APPLE CIDER

INGREDIENTS

- 1 cup pumpkin seeds
- 1 teaspoon cinnamon
- 2 packets stevia
- 1 tablespoon canola oil
- ¼ teaspoon sea salt

 **PREPARATION** 15 MIN    **COOKING** 3H    **SERVING** 4

DIRECTIONS

1. To make the spice bag, cut out a 6-inch square from double thick, pure cotton cheesecloth. Put in the cloves and cinnamon, then bring the corners up, tie it closed using a clean kitchen string that is pure cotton.
2. In a 3 1/2- 5-quart slow cooker, combine cranberry-raspberry juice, apple cider, and the spice bag.
3. Cook while covered over low heat setting for around 4-6 hours or on a high heat setting for 2-2 1/2 hours.
4. Throw out the spice bag. Serve right away or keep it warm while covered on warm or low-heat setting up to 2 hours, occasionally stirring. Garnish each serving with apples (thinly sliced).

Nutritions: *89 Calories, 22g Carbohydrates, 19g Sugar*

48. BRUNSWICK STEW

INGREDIENTS

- 4 ounces diced salt pork
- 2 pounds chicken parts
- 8 cups water
- 3 potatoes, cubed
- 3 onions, chopped
- 1 (28 ounce) can whole peeled tomatoes
- 2 cups canned whole kernel corn
- 1 (10 ounce) package frozen lima beans

- 1 tablespoon Worcestershire sauce
- 1/2 teaspoon salt
- 1/4 teaspoon ground black pepper

 **PREPARATION** 10 MIN

 **COOKING** 45 MIN

 **SERVING** 3

DIRECTIONS

1. Mix and boil water, chicken and salt pork in a big pot on high heat. Lower heat to low. Cover then simmer until chicken is tender for 45 minutes.
2. Take out chicken. Let cool until easily handled. Take meat out. Throw out bones and skin. Chop meat to bite-sized pieces. Put back in the soup.
3. Add ground black pepper, salt, Worcestershire sauce, lima beans, corn, tomatoes, onions and potatoes. Mix well. Stir well and simmer for 1 hour, uncovered.

Nutritions: *368 Calories, 25.9g Carbohydrate, 27.9g Protein*

49. BUFFALO CHICKEN SALADS

INGREDIENTS

- 1½ pounds chicken breast halves
- ½ cup Wing Time® Buffalo chicken sauce
- 4 teaspoons cider vinegar
- 1 teaspoon Worcestershire sauce
- 1 teaspoon paprika
- 1/3 cup light mayonnaise
- 2 tablespoons fat-free milk
- 2 tablespoons crumbled blue cheese
- 2 romaine hearts, chopped
- 1 cup whole grain croutons
- ½ cup very thinly sliced red onion

 **PREPARATION**
7 MIN

 **COOKING**
3H

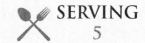 **SERVING**
5

DIRECTIONS

1. Place chicken in a 2-quarts slow cooker. Mix together Worcestershire sauce, 2 teaspoons of vinegar and Buffalo sauce in a small bowl; pour over chicken. Dust with paprika. Close and cook for 3 hours on low-heat setting.

2. Mix the leftover 2 teaspoons of vinegar with milk and light mayonnaise together in a small bowl at serving time; mix in blue cheese. While chicken is still in the slow cooker, pull meat into bite-sized pieces using two forks.

3. Split the romaine among 6 dishes.

Spoon sauce and chicken over lettuce. Pour with blue cheese dressing then add red onion slices and croutons on top.

Nutritions: *274 Calories, 11g Carbohydrate, 2g Fiber*

50. CACCIATORE STYLE CHICKEN

INGREDIENTS

- 2 cups sliced fresh mushrooms
- 1 cup sliced celery
- 1 cup chopped carrot
- 2 medium onions, cut into wedges
- 1 green, yellow, or red sweet peppers
- 4 cloves garlic, minced
- 12 chicken drumsticks
- ½ cup chicken broth
- ¼ cup dry white wine
- 2 tablespoons quick-cooking tapioca

- 2 bay leaves
- 1 teaspoon dried oregano, crushed
- 1 teaspoon sugar
- ½ teaspoon salt
- ¼ teaspoon pepper
- 1 (14.5 ounce) can diced tomatoes
- 1/3 cup tomato paste
- Hot cooked pasta or rice

 **PREPARATION** 10 MIN    **COOKING** 4H    **SERVING** 6

DIRECTIONS

1. Mix garlic, sweet pepper, onions, carrot, celery and mushrooms in a 5- or 6-qt. slow cooker. Cover veggies with the chicken. Add pepper, salt, sugar, oregano, bay leaves, tapioca, wine and broth.
2. Cover. Cook for 3–3 1/2 hours on high-heat setting.
3. Take chicken out; keep warm. Discard bay leaves. Turn to high-heat setting if using low-heat setting. Mix tomato paste and undrained tomatoes in. Cover. Cook on high-heat setting for 15 more minutes. Serving: Put veggie mixture on top of pasta and chicken.

Nutritions: *324 Calories, 7g Sugar:, 35g Carbohydrate*

51. CARNITAS TACOS

INGREDIENTS

- 3 to 3½-pound bone-in pork shoulder roast
- ½ cup chopped onion
- 1/3 cup orange juice
- 1 tablespoon ground cumin
- 1½ teaspoons kosher salt
- 1 teaspoon dried oregano, crushed
- ¼ teaspoon cayenne pepper
- 1 lime
- 2 (5.3 ounce) containers plain low-fat Greek yogurt
- 1 pinch kosher salt
- 16 (6 inch) soft yellow corn tortillas, such as Mission® brand
- 4 leaves green cabbage, quartered
- 1 cup very thinly sliced red onion
- 1 cup salsa (optional)

 **PREPARATION** 10 MIN    **COOKING** 5H    **SERVING** 4

DIRECTIONS

1. Take off meat from the bone; throw away bone. Trim meat fat. Slice meat into 2 to 3-inch pieces; put in a slow cooker of 3 1/2 or 4-quart in size. Mix in cayenne, oregano, salt, cumin, orange juice and onion.
2. Cover and cook for 4 to 5 hours on high. Take out meat from the cooker. Shred meat with two forks. Mix in enough cooking liquid to moisten.
3. Take out 1 teaspoon zest (put aside) for lime crema, then squeeze 2 tablespoons lime juice. Mix dash salt, yogurt, and lime juice in a small bowl.
4. Serve lime crema, salsa (if wished), red onion and cabbage with meat in tortillas. Scatter with lime zest.

Nutritions: *301 Calories, 28g Carbohydrate, 7g Sugar*

52. CHICKEN CHILI

INGREDIENTS

- 3 tablespoons vegetable oil
- 2 cloves garlic, minced
- 1 green bell pepper, chopped
- 1 onion, chopped
- 1 stalk celery, sliced
- 1/4-pound mushrooms, chopped
- 1-pound chicken breast
- 1 tablespoon chili powder
- 1 teaspoon dried oregano
- 1 teaspoon ground cumin

- 1/2 teaspoon paprika
- 1/2 teaspoon cocoa powder
- 1/4 teaspoon salt
- 1 pinch crushed red pepper flakes
- 1 pinch ground black pepper
- 1 (14.5 oz) can tomatoes with juice
- 1 (19 oz) can kidney beans

 **PREPARATION** 6 MIN

 **COOKING** 1H

 **SERVING** 4

DIRECTIONS

1. Fill 2 tablespoons of oil into a big skillet and heat it at moderate heat. Add mushrooms, celery, onion, bell pepper and garlic, sautéing for 5 minutes. Put it to one side.
2. Insert the leftover 1 tablespoon of oil into the skillet. At high heat, cook the chicken until browned and its exterior turns firm. Transfer the vegetable mixture back into skillet.
3. Stir in ground black pepper, hot pepper flakes, salt, cocoa powder, paprika, oregano, cumin and chili powder. Continue stirring for several minutes to avoid burning. Pour in the beans and tomatoes and lead the entire mixture to boiling point then adjust the setting to low heat. Place a lid on the skillet and leave it simmering for 15 minutes. Uncover the skillet and leave it simmering for another 15 minutes.

Nutritions: *308 Calories, 25.9g Carbohydrate, 29g Protein*

53. CHICKEN VERA CRUZ

INGREDIENTS

- 1 medium onion, cut into wedges
- 1-pound yellow-skin potatoes
- 6 skinless, boneless chicken thighs
- 2 (14.5 oz.) cans no-salt-added diced tomatoes
- 1 fresh jalapeño chili pepper
- 2 tablespoons Worcestershire sauce
- 1 tablespoon chopped garlic
- 1 teaspoon dried oregano, crushed
- ¼ teaspoon ground cinnamon
- 1/8 teaspoon ground cloves
- ½ cup snipped fresh parsley
- ¼ cup chopped pimiento-stuffed green olives

 **PREPARATION**
7 MIN

 **COOKING**
10 H

 **SERVING**
5

DIRECTIONS

1. Put onion in a 3 1/2- or 4-quart slow cooker. Place chicken thighs and potatoes on top. Drain and discard juices from a can of tomatoes. Stir undrained and drained tomatoes, cloves, cinnamon, oregano, garlic, Worcestershire sauce and jalapeño pepper together in a bowl. Pour over all in the cooker.
2. Cook with a cover for 10 hours on low-heat setting.
3. To make the topping: Stir chopped pimiento-stuffed green olives and snipped fresh parsley together in a small bowl. Drizzle the topping over each serving of chicken.

Nutritions: *228 Calories, 9g Sugar, 25g Carbohydrate*

54. CHICKEN AND CORNMEAL DUMPLINGS

INGREDIENTS

Chicken and Vegetable Filling
- 2 medium carrots, thinly sliced
- 1 stalk celery, thinly sliced
- 1/3 cup corn kernels
- ½ of a medium onion, thinly sliced
- 2 cloves garlic, minced
- 1 teaspoon snipped fresh rosemary
- ¼ teaspoon ground black pepper
- 2 chicken thighs, skinned
- 1 cup reduced sodium chicken broth

- ½ cup fat-free milk
- 1 tablespoon all-purpose flour

Cornmeal Dumplings
- ¼ cup flour
- ¼ cup cornmeal
- ½ teaspoon baking powder
- 1 egg white
- 1 tablespoon fat-free milk
- 1 tablespoon canola oil

 **PREPARATION** 8 MIN    **COOKING** 8 H    **SERVING** 4

DIRECTIONS

1. Mix 1/4 teaspoon pepper, carrots, garlic, celery, rosemary, corn, and onion in a 1 1/2 or 2-quart slow cooker. Place chicken on top. Pour the broth atop mixture in the cooker.
2. Close and cook on low-heat for 7 to 8 hours.
3. If cooking with the low-heat setting, switch to high-heat setting (or if heat setting is not available, continue to cook). Place the chicken onto a cutting board and let to cool slightly. Once cool enough to handle, chop off chicken from bones and get rid of the bones. Chop the chicken and place back into the mixture in cooker. Mix flour and milk in a small bowl until smooth. Stir into the mixture in

cooker.
4. Drop the Cornmeal Dumplings dough into 4 mounds atop hot chicken mixture using two spoons. Cover and cook for 20 to 25 minutes more or until a toothpick come out clean when inserted into a dumpling. (Avoid lifting lid when cooking.) Sprinkle each of the serving with coarse pepper if desired.
5. Mix together 1/2 teaspoon baking powder, 1/4 cup flour, a dash of salt and 1/4 cup cornmeal in a medium bowl. Mix 1 tablespoon canola oil, 1 egg white and 1 tablespoon fat-free milk in a small bowl. Pour the egg mixture into the flour mixture. Mix just until moistened.

Nutritions: *369 Calories, 9g Sugar, 47g Carbohydrate*

55. CHICKEN AND PEPPERONI

INGREDIENTS

- 3½ to 4 pounds meaty chicken pieces
- 1/8 teaspoon salt
- 1/8 teaspoon black pepper
- 2 ounces sliced turkey pepperoni
- ¼ cup sliced pitted ripe olives
- ½ cup reduced-sodium chicken broth
- 1 tablespoon tomato paste
- 1 teaspoon dried Italian seasoning,

- crushed
- ½ cup shredded part-skim mozzarella cheese (2 ounces)

 **PREPARATION** 4 MIN    **COOKING** 4 H    **SERVING** 5

DIRECTIONS

1. Put chicken into a 3 1/2 to 5-qt. slow cooker. Sprinkle pepper and salt on the chicken. Slice pepperoni slices in half. Put olives and pepperoni into the slow cooker. In a small bowl, blend Italian seasoning, tomato paste and chicken broth together. Transfer the mixture into the slow cooker.
2. Cook with a cover for 3-3 1/2 hours on high.
3. Transfer the olives, pepperoni and chicken onto a serving platter with a slotted spoon. Discard the cooking liquid. Sprinkle cheese over the chicken. Use foil to loosely cover and allow to sit for 5 minutes to melt the cheese.

Nutritions: *243 Calories, 1g Carbohydrate, 41g Protein*

56. CHICKEN AND SAUSAGE GUMBO

INGREDIENTS

- 1/3 cup all-purpose flour
- 1 (14 ounce) can reduced-sodium chicken broth
- 2 cups chicken breast
- 8 ounces smoked turkey sausage links
- 2 cups sliced fresh okra
- 1 cup water
- 1 cup coarsely chopped onion
- 1 cup sweet pepper

- ½ cup sliced celery
- 4 cloves garlic, minced
- 1 teaspoon dried thyme
- ½ teaspoon ground black pepper
- ¼ teaspoon cayenne pepper
- 3 cups hot cooked brown rice

 **PREPARATION** 6 MIN

 **COOKING** 4 H

 **SERVING** 5

DIRECTIONS

1. To make the roux: Cook the flour upon a medium heat in a heavy medium-sized saucepan, stirring periodically, for roughly 6 minutes or until the flour browns. Take off the heat and slightly cool, then slowly stir in the broth. Cook the roux until it bubbles and thickens up.
2. Pour the roux in a 3 1/2- or 4-quart slow cooker, then add in cayenne pepper, black pepper, thyme, garlic, celery, sweet pepper, onion, water, okra, sausage, and chicken.
3. Cook the soup covered on a high setting for 3 - 3 1/2 hours. Take the fat off the top and serve atop hot cooked brown rice.

Nutritions: *230 Calories, 3g Sugar, 19g Protein*

57. CHICKEN, BARLEY, AND LEEK STEW

INGREDIENTS

- 1-pound chicken thighs
- 1 tablespoon olive oil
- 1 (49 ounce) can reduced-sodium chicken broth
- 1 cup regular barley (not quick-cooking)
- 2 medium leeks, halved lengthwise and sliced
- 2 medium carrots, thinly sliced
- 1½ teaspoons dried basil or Italian seasoning, crushed
- ¼ teaspoon cracked black pepper

 **PREPARATION** 10 MIN

 **COOKING** 3 H

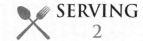 **SERVING** 2

DIRECTIONS

1. In the big skillet, cook the chicken in hot oil till becoming brown on all sides. In the 4-5-qt. slow cooker, whisk the pepper, dried basil, carrots, leeks, barley, chicken broth and chicken.

2. Keep covered and cooked over high heat setting for 2 – 2.5 hours or till the barley softens. As you wish, drizzle with the parsley or fresh basil prior to serving.

Nutritions: *248 Calories, 6g Fiber, 27g Carbohydrate*

58. CIDER PORK STEW

INGREDIENTS

- 2 pounds pork shoulder roast
- 3 medium cubed potatoes
- 3 medium carrots
- 2 medium onions, sliced
- 1 cup coarsely chopped apple
- ½ cup coarsely chopped celery
- 3 tablespoons quick-cooking tapioca
- 2 cups apple juice
- 1 teaspoon salt
- 1 teaspoon caraway seeds
- ¼ teaspoon black pepper

 PREPARATION 9 MIN

 **COOKING** 12 H

SERVING 3

DIRECTIONS

1. Chop the meat into 1-in. cubes. In the 3.5- 5.5 qt. slow cooker, mix the tapioca, celery, apple, onions, carrots, potatoes and meat. Whisk in pepper, caraway seeds, salt and apple juice.
2. Keep covered and cook over low heat setting for 10-12 hours. If you want, use the celery leaves to decorate each of the servings.

Nutritions: *244 Calories, 5g Fiber, 33g Carbohydrate*

59. CREAMY CHICKEN NOODLE SOUP

INGREDIENTS

- 1 (32 fluid ounce) container reduced-sodium chicken broth
- 3 cups water
- 2½ cups chopped cooked chicken
- 3 medium carrots, sliced
- 3 stalks celery
- 1½ cups sliced fresh mushrooms
- ¼ cup chopped onion
- 1½ teaspoons dried thyme, crushed
- ¾ teaspoon garlic-pepper seasoning
- 3 ounces reduced-fat cream cheese (Neufchâtel), cut up
- 2 cups dried egg noodles

 **PREPARATION** 7 MIN

 **COOKING** 8 H

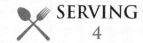 **SERVING** 4

DIRECTIONS

1. Mix together the garlic-pepper seasoning, thyme, onion, mushrooms, celery, carrots, chicken, water and broth in a 5 to 6-quart slow cooker.
2. Put cover and let it cook for 6-8 hours on low-heat setting.
3. Increase to high-heat setting if you are using low-heat setting. Mix in the cream cheese until blended. Mix in uncooked noodles. Put cover and let it cook for an additional 20-30 minutes or just until the noodles become tender.

Nutritions: *170 Calories, 3g Sugar, 2g Fiber*

60. CUBAN PULLED PORK SANDWICH

INGREDIENTS

- 1 teaspoon dried oregano, crushed
- ¾ teaspoon ground cumin
- ½ teaspoon ground coriander
- ¼ teaspoon salt
- ¼ teaspoon black pepper
- ¼ teaspoon ground allspice
- 1 2 to 2½-pound boneless pork shoulder roast
- 1 tablespoon olive oil
- Nonstick cooking spray
- 2 cups sliced onions
- 2 green sweet peppers, cut into bite-size strips
- ½ to 1 fresh jalapeño pepper
- 4 cloves garlic, minced
- ¼ cup orange juice
- ¼ cup lime juice
- 6 heart-healthy wheat hamburger buns, toasted
- 2 tablespoons jalapeño mustard

PREPARATION
6 MIN

COOKING
5 H

SERVING
5

DIRECTIONS

1. Mix allspice, oregano, black pepper, cumin, salt, and coriander together in a small bowl. Press each side of the roast into the spice mixture. On medium-high heat, heat oil in a big non-stick pan; put in roast. Cook for 5mins until both sides of the roast is light brown, turn the roast one time.

2. Using a cooking spray, grease a 3 1/2 or 4qt slow cooker; arrange the garlic, onions, jalapeno, and green peppers in a layer. Pour in lime juice and orange juice. Slice the roast if needed to fit inside the cooker; put on top of the vegetables covered or 4 1/2-5hrs on high heat setting.

3. Move roast to a cutting board using a slotted spoon. Drain the cooking liquid and keep the jalapeno, green peppers, and onions. Shred the roast with 2 forks then place it back in the cooker. Remove fat from the liquid. Mix half cup of cooking liquid and reserved vegetables into the cooker. Pour in more cooking liquid if desired. Discard the remaining cooking liquid.

4. Slather mustard on rolls. Split the meat between the bottom roll halves. Add avocado on top if desired. Place the roll tops to sandwiches.

Nutritions: *379 Calories, 32g Carbohydrate, 4g Fiber*

CHAPTER 4.
SECOND COURSE RECIPES

61. PORK CHOP DIANE

INGREDIENTS

- ¼ cup low-sodium chicken broth
- 1 tablespoon freshly squeezed lemon juice
- 2 teaspoons Worcestershire sauce
- 2 teaspoons Dijon mustard
- 4 (5-ounce) boneless pork top loin chops
- 1 teaspoon extra-virgin olive oil
- 1 teaspoon lemon zest
- 1 teaspoon butter

- 2 teaspoons chopped fresh chives

 **PREPARATION**
10 MIN

 **COOKING**
20 MIN

 **SERVING**
4

DIRECTIONS

1. Blend together the chicken broth, lemon juice, Worcestershire sauce, and Dijon mustard and set it aside.
2. Season the pork chops lightly.
3. Situate large skillet over medium-high heat and add the olive oil.
4. Cook the pork chops, turning once, until they are no longer pink, about 8 minutes per side.
5. Put aside the chops.
6. Pour the broth mixture into the skillet and cook until warmed through and thickened, about 2 minutes.
7. Blend lemon zest, butter, and chives.
8. Garnish with a generous spoonful of sauce.

Nutritions: *200 Calories, 8g Fat, 1g Carbohydrates*

62. AUTUMN PORK CHOPS WITH RED CABBAGE AND APPLES

INGREDIENTS

- ¼ cup apple cider vinegar
- 2 tablespoons granulated sweetener
- 4 (4-ounce) pork chops, about 1 inch thick
- 1 tablespoon extra-virgin olive oil
- ½ red cabbage, finely shredded
- 1 sweet onion, thinly sliced
- 1 apple, peeled, cored, and sliced
- 1 teaspoon chopped fresh thyme

 **PREPARATION** 15 MIN    **COOKING** 30 MIN    **SERVING** 4

DIRECTIONS

1. Scourge together the vinegar and sweetener. Set it aside.
2. Season the pork with salt and pepper.
3. Position huge skillet over medium-high heat and add the olive oil.
4. Cook the pork chops until no longer pink, turning once, about 8 minutes per side.
5. Put chops aside.
6. Add the cabbage and onion to the skillet and sauté until the vegetables have softened, about 5 minutes.
7. Add the vinegar mixture and the apple slices to the skillet and bring the mixture to a boil.
8. Adjust heat to low and simmer, covered, for 5 additional minutes.
9. Return the pork chops to the skillet, along with any accumulated juices and thyme, cover, and cook for 5 more minutes.

Nutritions: *223 Calories, 12g Carbohydrates, 3g Fiber*

63. CHIPOTLE CHILI PORK CHOPS

INGREDIENTS

- Juice and zest of 1 lime
- 1 tablespoon extra-virgin olive oil
- 1 tablespoon chipotle chili powder
- 2 teaspoons minced garlic
- 1 teaspoon ground cinnamon
- Pinch sea salt
- 4 (5-ounce) pork chops

 **PREPARATION** 4 H

 **COOKING** 20 MIN

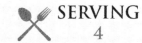 **SERVING** 4

DIRECTIONS

1. Combine the lime juice and zest, oil, chipotle chili powder, garlic, cinnamon, and salt in a resealable plastic bag. Add the pork chops. Remove as much air as possible and seal the bag.
2. Marinate the chops in the refrigerator for at least 4 hours, and up to 24 hours, turning them several times.
3. Ready the oven to 400°F and set a rack on a baking sheet. Let the chops rest at room temperature for 15 minutes, then arrange them on the rack and discard the remaining marinade.
4. Roast the chops until cooked through, turning once, about 10 minutes per side.
5. Serve with lime wedges.

Nutritions: *204 Calories, 1g Carbohydrates, 1g Sugar*

64. ORANGE-MARINATED PORK TENDERLOIN

INGREDIENTS

- ¼ cup freshly squeezed orange juice
- 2 teaspoons orange zest
- 2 teaspoons minced garlic
- 1 teaspoon low-sodium soy sauce
- 1 teaspoon grated fresh ginger
- 1 teaspoon honey
- 1½ pounds pork tenderloin roast
- 1 tablespoon extra-virgin olive oil

 **PREPARATION** 2 H    **COOKING** 30 MIN    **SERVING** 4

DIRECTIONS

1. Blend together the orange juice, zest, garlic, soy sauce, ginger, and honey.
2. Pour the marinade into a resealable plastic bag and add the pork tenderloin.
3. Remove as much air as possible and seal the bag. Marinate the pork in the refrigerator, turning the bag a few times, for 2 hours.
4. Preheat the oven to 400°F.
5. Pull out tenderloin from the marinade and discard the marinade.
6. Position big ovenproof skillet over medium-high heat and add the oil.
7. Sear the pork tenderloin on all sides, about 5 minutes in total.
8. Position skillet to the oven and roast for 25 minutes.
9. Put aside for 10 minutes before serving.

Nutritions: *228 Calories, 4g Carbohydrates, 3g Sugar*

65. HOMESTYLE HERB MEATBALLS

INGREDIENTS

- ½ pound lean ground pork
- ½ pound lean ground beef
- 1 sweet onion, finely chopped
- ¼ cup bread crumbs
- 2 tablespoons chopped fresh basil
- 2 teaspoons minced garlic
- 1 egg

 **PREPARATION**
10 MIN

 **COOKING**
15 MIN

 **SERVING**
4

DIRECTIONS

1. Preheat the oven to 350°F.
2. Ready baking tray with parchment paper and set it aside.
3. In a large bowl, mix together the pork, beef, onion, bread crumbs, basil, garlic, egg, salt, and pepper until very well mixed.
4. Roll the meat mixture into 2-inch meatballs.
5. Transfer the meatballs to the baking sheet and bake until they are browned and cooked through, about 15 minutes.
6. Serve the meatballs with your favorite marinara sauce and some steamed green beans.

Nutritions: *332 Calories, 13g Carbohydrates, 3g Sugar*

66. LIME-PARSLEY LAMB CUTLETS

INGREDIENTS

- ¼ cup extra-virgin olive oil
- ¼ cup freshly squeezed lime juice
- 2 tablespoons lime zest
- 2 tablespoons chopped fresh parsley
- 12 lamb cutlets (about 1½ pounds total)

 **PREPARATION** 4 H

 **COOKING** 10 MIN

 **SERVING** 4

DIRECTIONS

1. Scourge the oil, lime juice, zest, parsley, salt, and pepper.
2. Pour marinade to a resealable plastic bag.
3. Add the cutlets to the bag and remove as much air as possible before sealing.
4. Marinate the lamb in the refrigerator for about 4 hours, turning the bag several times.
5. Preheat the oven to broil.
6. Remove the chops from the bag and arrange them on an aluminum foil–lined baking sheet. Discard the marinade.
7. Broil the chops for 4 minutes per side for medium doneness.
8. Let the chops rest for 5 minutes before serving.

Nutritions: *413 Calories, 1g Carbohydrates, 31g Protein*

67. MEDITERRANEAN STEAK SANDWICHES

INGREDIENTS

- 2 tablespoons extra-virgin olive oil
- 2 tablespoons balsamic vinegar
- 2 teaspoons garlic
- 2 teaspoons lemon juice
- 2 teaspoons fresh oregano
- 1 teaspoon fresh parsley
- 1-pound flank steak
- 4 whole-wheat pitas
- 2 cups shredded lettuce
- 1 red onion, thinly sliced
- 1 tomato, chopped
- 1 ounce low-sodium feta cheese

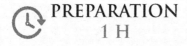 **PREPARATION**
1 H

 **COOKING**
10 MIN

 **SERVING**
4

DIRECTIONS

1. Scourge olive oil, balsamic vinegar, garlic, lemon juice, oregano, and parsley.
2. Add the steak to the bowl, turning to coat it completely.
3. Marinate the steak for 1 hour in the refrigerator, turning it over several times.
4. Preheat the broiler. Line a baking sheet with aluminum foil.
5. Put steak out of the bowl and discard the marinade.
6. Situate steak on the baking sheet and broil for 5 minutes per side for medium.
7. Set aside for 10 minutes before slicing.
8. Stuff the pitas with the sliced steak, lettuce, onion, tomato, and feta.

Nutritions: *344 Calories, 22g Carbohydrates, 3g Fiber*

68. ROASTED BEEF WITH PEPPERCORN SAUCE

INGREDIENTS

- 1½ pounds top rump beef roast
- 3 teaspoons extra-virgin olive oil
- 3 shallots, minced
- 2 teaspoons minced garlic
- 1 tablespoon green peppercorns
- 2 tablespoons dry sherry
- 2 tablespoons all-purpose flour
- 1 cup sodium-free beef broth

 **PREPARATION** 10 MIN
 **COOKING** 90 MIN
 **SERVING** 4

DIRECTIONS

1. Heat the oven to 300°F.
2. Season the roast with salt and pepper.
3. Position huge skillet over medium-high heat and add 2 teaspoons of olive oil.
4. Brown the beef on all sides, about 10 minutes in total, and transfer the roast to a baking dish.
5. Roast until desired doneness, about 1½ hours for medium. When the roast has been in the oven for 1 hour, start the sauce.
6. In a medium saucepan over medium-high heat, sauté the shallots in the remaining 1 teaspoon of olive oil until translucent, about 4 minutes.
7. Stir in the garlic and peppercorns, and cook for another minute. Whisk in the sherry to deglaze the pan.
8. Whisk in the flour to form a thick paste, cooking for 1 minute and stirring constantly.
9. Fill in the beef broth and whisk for 4 minutes. Season the sauce.
10. Serve the beef with a generous spoonful of sauce.

Nutritions: *330 Calories, 4g Carbohydrates, 36g Protein*

69. COFFEE-AND-HERB-MARINATED STEAK

INGREDIENTS

- ¼ cup whole coffee beans
- 2 teaspoons garlic
- 2 teaspoons rosemary
- 2 teaspoons thyme
- 1 teaspoon black pepper
- 2 tablespoons apple cider vinegar
- 2 tablespoons extra-virgin olive oil
- 1-pound flank steak, trimmed of visible fat

 **PREPARATION**
2 H

 **COOKING**
10MIN

 **SERVING**
3

DIRECTIONS

1. Place the coffee beans, garlic, rosemary, thyme, and black pepper in a coffee grinder or food processor and pulse until coarsely ground.
2. Transfer the coffee mixture to a resealable plastic bag and add the vinegar and oil. Shake to combine.
3. Add the flank steak and squeeze the excess air out of the bag. Seal it. Marinate the steak in the refrigerator for at least 2 hours, occasionally turning the bag over.
4. Preheat the broiler. Line a baking sheet with aluminum foil.
5. Pull the steak out and discard the marinade.
6. Position steak on the baking sheet and broil until it is done to your liking.
7. Put aside for 10 minutes before cutting it.
8. Serve with your favorite side dish.

Nutritions: *313 Calories, 20g Fat, 31g Protein*

70. TRADITIONAL BEEF STROGANOFF

INGREDIENTS

- 1 teaspoon extra-virgin olive oil
- 1-pound top sirloin, cut into thin strips
- 1 cup sliced button mushrooms
- ½ sweet onion, finely chopped
- 1 teaspoon minced garlic
- 1 tablespoon whole-wheat flour
- ½ cup low-sodium beef broth
- ¼ cup dry sherry
- ½ cup fat-free sour cream

- 1 tablespoon chopped fresh parsley

 **PREPARATION** 10 MIN

 **COOKING** 30 MIN

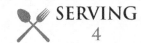 **SERVING** 4

DIRECTIONS

1. Position the skillet over medium-high heat and add the oil.
2. Sauté the beef until browned, about 10 minutes, then remove the beef with a slotted spoon to a plate and set it aside.
3. Add the mushrooms, onion, and garlic to the skillet and sauté until lightly browned, about 5 minutes.
4. Whisk in the flour and then whisk in the beef broth and sherry.
5. Return the sirloin to the skillet and bring the mixture to a boil.
6. Reduce the heat to low and simmer until the beef is tender, about 10 minutes.
7. Stir in the sour cream and parsley. Season with salt and pepper.

Nutritions: *257 Calories, 6g Carbohydrates, 1g Fiber*

71. CHICKEN AND ROASTED VEGETABLE WRAPS

INGREDIENTS

- ½ small eggplant
- 1 red bell pepper
- 1 medium zucchini
- ½ small red onion, sliced
- 1 tablespoon extra-virgin olive oil
- 2 (8-ounce) cooked chicken breasts, sliced
- 4 whole-wheat tortilla wraps

 **PREPARATION** 10 MIN    **COOKING** 20 MIN   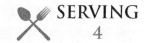 **SERVING** 4

DIRECTIONS

1. Preheat the oven to 400°F.
2. Wrap baking sheet with foil and set it aside.
3. In a large bowl, toss the eggplant, bell pepper, zucchini, and red onion with the olive oil.
4. Transfer the vegetables to the baking sheet and lightly season with salt and pepper.
5. Roast the vegetables until soft and slightly charred, about 20 minutes.
6. Divide the vegetables and chicken into four portions.
7. Wrap 1 tortilla around each portion of chicken and grilled vegetables, and serve.

Nutritions: *483 Calories, 45g Carbohydrates, 3g Fiber*

72. SPICY CHICKEN CACCIATORE

INGREDIENTS

- 1 (2-pound) chicken
- ¼ cup all-purpose flour
- 2 tablespoons extra-virgin olive oil
- 3 slices bacon
- 1 sweet onion
- 2 teaspoons minced garlic
- 4 ounces button mushrooms, halved
- 1 (28-ounce) can low-sodium stewed tomatoes
- ½ cup red wine

- 2 teaspoons chopped fresh oregano

 **PREPARATION** 20 MIN    **COOKING** 1 H    **SERVING** 6

DIRECTIONS

1. Cut the chicken into pieces: 2 drumsticks, 2 thighs, 2 wings, and 4 breast pieces.
2. Dredge the chicken pieces in the flour and season each piece with salt and pepper.
3. Place a large skillet over medium-high heat and add the olive oil.
4. Brown the chicken pieces on all sides, about 20 minutes in total. Transfer the chicken to a plate.
5. Cook chopped bacon to the skillet for 5 minutes. With a slotted spoon, transfer the cooked bacon to the same plate as the chicken.
6. Pour off most of the oil from the skillet, leaving just a light coating. Sauté the onion, garlic, and mushrooms in the skillet until tender, about 4 minutes.
7. Stir in the tomatoes, wine, oregano, and red pepper flakes.
8. Bring the sauce to a boil. Return the chicken and bacon, plus any accumulated juices from the plate, to the skillet.
9. Reduce the heat to low and simmer until the chicken is tender, about 30 minutes.

Nutritions: *230 Calories, 14g Carbohydrates, 2g Fiber*

73. GINGER CITRUS CHICKEN THIGHS

INGREDIENTS

- 4 chicken thighs, bone-in, skinless
- 1 tablespoon grated fresh ginger
- 1 tablespoon extra-virgin olive oil
- Juice and zest of ½ lemon
- Juice and zest of ½ orange
- 2 tablespoons honey
- 1 tablespoon reduced-sodium soy sauce
- 1 tablespoon chopped fresh cilantro

 **PREPARATION** 15 MIN    **COOKING** 30 MIN    **SERVING** 4

DIRECTIONS

1. Rub the chicken thighs with the ginger and season lightly with salt.
2. Place a large skillet over medium-high heat and add the oil.
3. Brown the chicken thighs, turning once, for about 10 minutes.
4. While the chicken is browning, stir together the lemon juice and zest, orange juice and zest, honey, soy sauce, and red pepper flakes in a small bowl.
5. Add the citrus mixture to the skillet, cover, and reduce the heat to low.
6. Braise chicken for 20 minutes, adding a couple of tablespoons of water if the pan is too dry.
7. Serve garnished with the cilantro.

Nutritions: 114 Calories, 9g Carbohydrates, 9g Protein

74. CHICKEN WITH CREAMY THYME SAUCE

INGREDIENTS

- 4 (4-ounce) chicken breasts
- 1 tablespoon extra-virgin olive oil
- ½ sweet onion, chopped
- 1 cup low-sodium chicken broth
- 2 teaspoons chopped fresh thyme
- ¼ cup heavy (whipping) cream
- 1 tablespoon butter
- 1 scallion

 **PREPARATION** 15 MIN    **COOKING** 30 MIN    **SERVING** 4

DIRECTIONS

1. Preheat the oven to 375°F.
2. Season the chicken breasts slightly.
3. Position large ovenproof skillet over medium-high heat and add the olive oil.
4. Brown the chicken, turning once, about 10 minutes in total. Transfer the chicken to a plate.
5. In the same skillet, sauté the onion until softened and translucent, about 3 minutes.
6. Add the chicken broth and thyme, and simmer until the liquid has reduced by half, about 6 minutes.
7. Stir in the cream and butter, and return the chicken and any accumulated juices from the plate to the skillet.
8. Transfer the skillet to the oven. Bake until cooked through, about 10 minutes.
9. Serve topped with the chopped scallion.

Nutritions: *287 Calories, 4g Carbohydrates, 1g Fiber*

75. ONE-POT ROAST CHICKEN DINNER

INGREDIENTS

- ½ head cabbage
- 1 sweet onion
- 1 sweet potato
- 4 garlic cloves
- 2 tablespoons extra-virgin olive oil
- 2 teaspoons minced fresh thyme
- 2½ pounds bone-in chicken thighs and drumsticks

 **PREPARATION** 10 MIN

 **COOKING** 40 MIN

 **SERVING** 6

DIRECTIONS

1. Preheat the oven to 450°F.
2. Lightly grease a large roasting pan and arrange the cabbage, onion, sweet potato, and garlic in the bottom. Drizzle with 1 tablespoon of oil, sprinkle with the thyme, and season the vegetables lightly with salt and pepper.
3. Season the chicken with salt and pepper.
4. Place a large skillet over medium-high heat and brown the chicken on both sides in the remaining 1 tablespoon of oil, about 10 minutes in total.
5. Situate browned chicken on top of the vegetables in the roasting pan. Roast for 30 minutes.

Nutritions: *540 Calories, 14g Carbohydrates, 4g Fiber*

76. ALMOND-CRUSTED SALMON

INGREDIENTS

- ¼ cup almond meal
- ¼ cup whole-wheat breadcrumbs
- ¼ teaspoon ground coriander
- 1/8 teaspoon ground cumin
- 4 (6-ounce) boneless salmon fillets
- 1 tablespoon fresh lemon juice
- Salt and pepper

 **PREPARATION** 10 MIN    **COOKING** 15 MIN    **SERVING** 4

DIRECTIONS

1. Ready the oven at 500°F and line a small baking dish with foil.
2. Combine the almond meal, breadcrumbs, coriander, and cumin in a small bowl.
3. Rinse the fish in cool water then pat dry and brush with lemon juice.
4. Season the fish with salt and pepper then dredge in the almond mixture on both sides.
5. Situate fish in the baking dish and bake for 15 minutes.

Nutritions: *232 Calories, 5.8g Carbohydrates, 1.7g Sugar:*

77. CHICKEN & VEGGIE BOWL WITH BROWN RICE

INGREDIENTS

- 1 cup instant brown rice
- ¼ cup tahini
- ¼ cup fresh lemon juice
- 2 cloves minced garlic
- ¼ teaspoon ground cumin
- Pinch salt
- 1 tablespoon olive oil
- 4 (4-ounce) chicken breast halves
- ½ medium yellow onion, sliced
- 1 cup green beans, trimmed
- 1 cup chopped broccoli
- 4 cups chopped kale

 **PREPARATION** 10 MIN    **COOKING** 20 MIN    **SERVING** 4

DIRECTIONS

1. Bring 1-cup water to boil in a small saucepan.
2. Stir in the brown rice and simmer for 5 minutes then cover and set aside.
3. Meanwhile, whisk together the tahini with ¼-cup water in a small bowl.
4. Stir in the lemon juice, garlic, and cumin with a pinch of salt and stir well.
5. Heat up oil in a big cast-iron skillet over medium heat.
6. Season the chicken with salt and pepper then add to the skillet.
7. Cook for 3 to 5 minutes on each side until cooked through then remove to a cutting board and cover loosely with foil.
8. Reheat the skillet and cook the onion for 2 minutes then stir in the broccoli and beans.
9. Sauté for 2 minutes then stir in the kale and sauté 2 minutes more.
10. Add 2 tablespoons of water then cover and steam for 2 minutes while you slice the chicken.
11. Build the bowls with brown rice, sliced chicken, and sautéed veggies.
12. Serve hot drizzled with the lemon tahini dressing.

Nutritions: *435 Calories, 24g Carbohydrates, 4.8g Fiber*

78. BEEF FAJITAS

INGREDIENTS

- 1 lbs. lean beef sirloin, sliced thin
- 1 tablespoon olive oil
- 1 medium red onion, sliced
- 1 red pepper, sliced thin
- 1 green pepper, sliced thin
- ½ teaspoon ground cumin
- ½ teaspoon chili powder
- 8 (6-inch) whole-wheat tortillas
- Fat-free sour cream

 **PREPARATION** 10 MIN  **COOKING** 15 MIN  **SERVING** 4

DIRECTIONS

1. Preheat huge cast-iron skillet over medium heat then add the oil.
2. Add the sliced beef and cook in a single layer for 1 minute on each side.
3. Remove the beef to a bowl and cover to keep warm.
4. Reheat the skillet then add the onions and peppers – season with cumin and chili powder.
5. Stir-fry the veggies to your liking then add to the bowl with the beef.
6. Serve hot in small whole-wheat tortillas with sliced avocado and fat-free sour cream.

Nutritions: *430 Calories, 30.5g Carbohydrates, 17g Fiber*

79. ITALIAN PORK CHOPS

INGREDIENTS

- 4 pork chops, boneless
- 3 garlic cloves, minced
- 1 tsp. dried rosemary, crushed
- ¼ tsp. pepper
- ¼ tsp. sea salt

 **PREPARATION**
5 MIN

 **COOKING**
45 MIN

 **SERVING**
4

DIRECTIONS

1. Prepare the oven to 425 F/ 218 C.
2. Line baking tray with cooking spray and season pork chops with pepper and salt.
3. Combine garlic and rosemary and rub all over pork chops.
4. Place pork chops in a prepared baking tray.
5. Roast pork chops in preheated oven for 10 minutes.
6. Set temperature to 180 C and roast for 25 minutes.
7. Serve and enjoy

Nutritions: *261 Calories, 1g Carbohydrates, 18g Protein*

80. CHICKEN MUSHROOM STROGANOFF

INGREDIENTS

- 1 cup fat-free sour cream
- 2 tablespoons flour
- 1 tablespoon Worcestershire sauce
- ½ teaspoon dried thyme
- 1 chicken bouillon cube, crushed
- Salt and pepper
- ½ cup water
- 1 medium yellow onion
- 8 ounces sliced mushrooms
- 1 tablespoon olive oil
- 2 cloves minced garlic
- 12 ounces chicken breast
- 6 ounces whole-wheat noodles, cooked

 **PREPARATION** 5 MIN

 **COOKING** 25 MIN

 **SERVING** 6

DIRECTIONS

1. Whisk together 2/3 cup of the sour cream with the flour, Worcestershire sauce, thyme, and crushed bouillon in a medium bowl.
2. Season with salt and pepper then slowly stir in the water until well combined.
3. Cook oil in a large skillet over medium-high heat.
4. Sauté onions, mushrooms for 3 minutes.
5. Cook garlic for 2 minutes more then add the chicken.
6. Pour in the sour cream mixture and cook until thick and bubbling.
7. Reduce heat and simmer for 2 minutes.
8. Spoon the chicken and mushroom mixture over the cooked noodles and garnish with the remaining sour cream to serve.

Nutritions: *295 Calories, 29.6g Carbohydrates, 2.9g Fiber*

81. GRILLED TUNA KEBABS

INGREDIENTS

- 2 ½ tablespoons rice vinegar
- 2 tablespoons fresh grated ginger
- 2 tablespoons sesame oil
- 2 tablespoons soy sauce
- 2 tablespoons fresh chopped cilantro
- 1 tablespoon minced green chili
- 1 ½ pounds fresh tuna
- 1 large red pepper
- 1 large red onion

 **PREPARATION** 20 MIN    **COOKING** 10 MIN   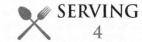 **SERVING** 4

DIRECTIONS

1. Whisk together the rice vinegar, ginger, sesame oil, soy sauce, cilantro, and chili in a medium bowl – add a few drops of liquid stevia extract to sweeten.
2. Toss in the tuna and chill for 20 minutes, covered.
3. Meanwhile, grease a grill pan with cooking spray and soak wooden skewers in water.
4. Slide the tuna cubes onto the skewers with red pepper and onion.
5. Grill for 4 minutes per side and serve hot.

Nutritions: *240 Calories, 8.5g Carbohydrates, 1.7g Fiber*

82. CAST-IRON PORK LOIN

INGREDIENTS

- 1 (1 ½ pounds) boneless pork loin
- Salt and pepper
- 2 tablespoons olive oil
- 2 tablespoons dried herb blend

 **PREPARATION** 10 MIN  **COOKING** 20 MIN  **SERVING** 6

DIRECTIONS

1. Heat the oven to 425°F.
2. Cut the excess fat from the pork and season.
3. Heat the oil in a large cast-iron skillet over medium heat.
4. Add the pork and cook for 2 minutes on each side.
5. Sprinkle the herbs over the pork and transfer to the oven.
6. Roast for 10 to 15 minutes.
7. Put aside for 10 minutes before cutting to serve.

Nutritions: *205 Calories, 1g Carbohydrates, 29g Protein*

83. CRISPY BAKED TOFU

INGREDIENTS

- 1 (14-ounce) block extra-firm tofu
- 1 tablespoon olive oil
- 1 tablespoon cornstarch
- ½ teaspoon garlic powder
- Salt and pepper

 **PREPARATION**
5 MIN

 **COOKING**
25 MIN

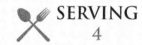 **SERVING**
4

DIRECTIONS

1. Spread paper towels out on a flat surface.
2. Cut the tofu into slices up to about ½-inch thick and lay them out.
3. Cover the tofu with another paper towel and place a cutting board on top.
4. Let the tofu drain for 10 to 15 minutes.
5. Preheat the oven to 400°F and line a baking sheet with foil or parchment.
6. Slice tofu into cubes and situate in a large bowl.
7. Toss with the olive oil, cornstarch, and garlic powder, salt and pepper.
8. Spread on the baking sheet and bake for 10 minutes.
9. Flip the tofu and bake for another 10 to 15 minutes. Serve hot.

Nutritions: *140 Calories, 2.1g Carbohydrates, 0.1g Fiber*

84. TILAPIA WITH COCONUT RICE

INGREDIENTS

- 4 (6-ounce) boneless tilapia fillets
- 1 tablespoon ground turmeric
- 1 tablespoon olive oil
- 2 (8.8-ounce) packets precooked whole-grain rice
- 1 cup light coconut milk
- ½ cup fresh chopped cilantro
- 1 ½ tablespoons fresh lime juice

 **PREPARATION** 10 MIN

 **COOKING** 15 MIN

 **SERVING** 4

DIRECTIONS

1. Season the fish with turmeric, salt, and pepper.
2. Cook oil in a large skillet at medium heat and add the fish.
3. Cook for 2 to 3 minutes per side until golden brown.
4. Remove the fish to a plate and cover to keep warm.
5. Reheat the skillet and add the rice, coconut milk, and a pinch of salt.
6. Simmer on high heat until thickened, about 3 to 4 minutes.
7. Stir in the cilantro and lime juice.
8. Spoon the rice onto plates and serve with the cooked fish.

Nutritions: *460 Calories, 27.1g Carbohydrates, 3.7g Fiber*

85. SPICY TURKEY TACOS

INGREDIENTS

- 1 tablespoon olive oil
- 1 medium yellow onion, diced
- 2 cloves minced garlic
- 1 pound 93% lean ground turkey
- 1 cup tomato sauce, no sugar added
- 1 jalapeno, seeded and minced
- 8 low-carb multigrain tortillas

 **PREPARATION**
5 MIN

 **COOKING**
25 MIN

 **SERVING**
8

DIRECTIONS

1. Heat up oil in a big skillet over medium heat.
2. Add the onion and sauté for 4 minutes then stir in the garlic and cook 1 minute more.
3. Stir in the ground turkey and cook for 5 minutes until browned, breaking it up with a wooden spoon.
4. Sprinkle on the taco seasoning and cayenne then stir well.
5. Cook for 30 seconds and mix in the tomato sauce and jalapeno.
6. Simmer on low heat for 10 minutes while you warm the tortillas in the microwave.
7. Serve the meat in the tortillas with your favorite taco toppings.

Nutritions: *195 Calories, 15.4g Carbohydrates, 8g Fiber*

86. QUICK AND EASY SHRIMP STIR-FRY

INGREDIENTS

- 1 tablespoon olive oil
- 1-pound uncooked shrimp
- 1 tablespoon sesame oil
- 8 ounces snow peas
- 4 ounces broccoli, chopped
- 1 medium red pepper, sliced
- 3 cloves minced garlic
- 1 tablespoon fresh grated ginger
- ½ cup soy sauce
- 1 tablespoon cornstarch

- 2 tablespoons fresh lime juice
- ¼ teaspoon liquid stevia extract

 **PREPARATION** 15 MIN    **COOKING** 15 MIN   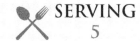 **SERVING** 5

DIRECTIONS

1. Cook olive oil in a huge skillet over medium heat.
2. Add the shrimp and season then sauté for 5 minutes.
3. Remove the shrimp to a bowl and keep warm.
4. Reheat the skillet with the sesame oil and add the veggies.
5. Sauté until the veggies are tender, about 6 to 8 minutes.
6. Cook garlic and ginger for 1 minute more.
7. Whisk together the remaining ingredients and pour into the skillet.
8. Toss to coat the veggies then add the shrimp and reheat. Serve hot.

Nutritions: *220 Calories, 12.7g Carbohydrates, 2.6g Fiber*

87. CHICKEN BURRITO BOWL WITH QUINOA

INGREDIENTS

- 1 tablespoon chipotle chills in adobo
- 1 tablespoon olive oil
- ½ teaspoon garlic powder
- ½ teaspoon ground cumin
- 1-pound boneless skinless chicken breast
- 2 cups cooked quinoa
- 2 cups shredded romaine lettuce
- 1 cup black beans
- 1 cup diced avocado
- 3 tablespoons fat-free sour cream

 **PREPARATION** 15 MIN

 **COOKING** 10 MIN

 **SERVING** 6

DIRECTIONS

1. Stir together the chipotle chills, olive oil, garlic powder, and cumin in a small bowl.
2. Preheat a grill pan to medium-high and grease with cooking spray.
3. Season the chicken with salt and pepper and add to the grill pan.
4. Grill for 5 minutes then flip it and brush with the chipotle glaze.
5. Cook for another 3 to 5 minutes until cooked through.
6. Remove to a cutting board and chop the chicken.
7. Assemble the bowls with 1/6 of the quinoa, chicken, lettuce, beans, and avocado.
8. Top each with a half tablespoon of fat-free sour cream to serve.

Nutritions: 410 Calories, 37.4g Carbohydrates, 8.5g Fiber

88. BAKED SALMON CAKES

INGREDIENTS

- 15 ounces canned salmon, drained
- 1 large egg, whisked
- 2 teaspoons Dijon mustard
- 1 small yellow onion, minced
- 1 ½ cups whole-wheat breadcrumbs
- ¼ cup low-fat mayonnaise
- ¼ cup nonfat Greek yogurt, plain
- 1 tablespoon fresh chopped parsley
- 1 tablespoon fresh lemon juice
- 2 green onions, sliced thin

 **PREPARATION** 10 MIN

 **COOKING** 20 MIN

 **SERVING** 4

DIRECTIONS

1. Set the oven to 450°F and prep baking sheet with parchment.
2. Flake the salmon into a medium bowl then stir in the egg and mustard.
3. Mix in the onions and breadcrumbs by hand, blending well, then shape into 8 patties.
4. Grease a large skillet and heat it over medium heat.
5. Fry patties for 2 minutes per side.
6. Situate patties to the baking sheet and bake for 15 minutes.
7. Meanwhile, whisk together the remaining ingredients.
8. Serve the baked salmon cakes with the creamy herb sauce.

Nutritions: *240 Calories, 9.3g Carbohydrates, 1.5g Fiber*

89. RICE AND MEATBALL STUFFED BELL PEPPERS

INGREDIENTS

- 4 bell peppers
- 1-tablespoon olive oil
- 1 small onion, chopped
- 2 cloves garlic, minced
- 1 cup frozen cooked rice, thawed
- 16 to 20 small frozen precooked meatballs
- ½-cup tomato sauce
- 2 tablespoons Dijon mustard

 **PREPARATION**
15 MIN

 **COOKING**
20 MIN

 **SERVING**
4

DIRECTIONS

1. To prepare the peppers, cut off about ½ inch of the tops. Carefully take out membranes and seeds from inside the peppers. Set aside.
2. In a 6-by-6-by-2-inch pan, combine the olive oil, onion, and garlic. Bake in the air fryer for 2 to 4 minutes or until crisp and tender. Remove the vegetable mixture from the pan and set aside in a medium bowl.
3. Add the rice, meatballs, tomato sauce, and mustard to the vegetable mixture and stir to combine
4. Stuff the peppers with the meat-vegetable mixture.
5. Situate peppers in the air fryer basket and bake for 9 to 13 minutes or until the filling is hot and the peppers are tender.

Nutritions: 487 Calories, 57g Carbohydrates, 6g Fiber

90. STIR-FRIED STEAK AND CABBAGE

INGREDIENTS

- ½-pound sirloin steak, cut into strips
- 2 teaspoons cornstarch
- 1-tablespoon peanut oil
- 2 cups chopped red or green cabbage
- 1 yellow bell pepper, chopped
- 2 green onions, chopped
- 2 cloves garlic, sliced
- ½-cup commercial stir-fry sauce

 **PREPARATION** 15 MIN    **COOKING** 10 MIN    **SERVING** 4

DIRECTIONS

1. Toss the steak with the cornstarch and set aside
2. In a 6-inch metal bowl, combine the peanut oil with the cabbage. Place in the basket and cook for 3 to 4 minutes.
3. Remove the bowl from the basket and add the steak, pepper, onions, and garlic. Return to the air fryer and cook for 3 to 5 minutes.
4. Add the stir-fry sauce and cook for 2 to 4 minutes. Serve over rice.

Nutritions: *180 Calories, 9g Carbohydrates, 2g Fiber*

91. LEMON CHICKEN WITH PEPPERS

INGREDIENTS

- 1 tsp cornstarch
- 1 tbsp. low sodium soy sauce
- 12 oz. chicken breast tenders, cut in thirds
- 1/4 cup fresh lemon juice
- 1/4 cup low sodium soy sauce
- 1/4 cup fat-free chicken broth
- 1 tsp. fresh ginger, minced
- 2 cloves garlic, minced
- 1 tablespoon Splenda

- 1 teaspoon cornstarch
- 1 tablespoon vegetable oil
- 1/4 cup red bell pepper
- 1/4 cup green bell pepper

 **PREPARATION**
5 MIN

 **COOKING**
20 MIN

 **SERVING**
6

DIRECTIONS

1. Scourge 1 teaspoon cornstarch and 1 tablespoon soy sauce. Add sliced chicken tenders. Chill to marinate for 10 minutes.
2. Stir the lemon juice, 1/4 cup soy sauce, chicken broth, ginger, garlic, Splenda and 1 teaspoon cornstarch together.
3. Warm up oil in a medium frying pan. Cook chicken over medium-high heat for 4 minutes.
4. Add sauce and sliced peppers. Cook 1 to 2 minutes more.

Nutritions: *150 calories, 1g fiber, 6g carbohydrates*

92. DIJON HERB CHICKEN

INGREDIENTS

- 4 skinless, boneless chicken breast halves
- 1 tablespoon butter
- 1 tablespoon olive or vegetable oil
- 2 garlic cloves, finely minced
- 1/2 cup dry white wine
- 1/4 cup water
- 2 tablespoons Dijon-style mustard
- 1/2 teaspoon dried dill weed
- 1/4 teaspoon coarsely ground pepper

- 1/3 cups chopped fresh parsley

PREPARATION 7 MIN

COOKING 25 MIN

SERVING 4

DIRECTIONS

1. Situate chicken breasts between sheets of plastic wrap or waxed paper, and pound with a kitchen mallet until they are evenly about 1/4-inch thick.
2. Warm up butter and oil over medium-high heat; cook chicken pieces for 3 minutes per side. Transfer chicken to a platter; keep warm and set aside.
3. Sauté garlic for 15 seconds in skillet drippings; stir in wine, water, mustard, dill weed, salt and pepper. Boil and reduce volume by 1/2, stirring up the browned bits at the bottom of the skillet.
4. Drizzle sauce over chicken cutlets. Sprinkle with parsley and serve.

Nutritions: *223 calories, 1g fiber, 6g carbohydrates*

93. SESAME CHICKEN STIR FRY

INGREDIENTS

- 12 ounces skinless, boneless chicken breast
- 1 tablespoon vegetable oil
- 2 garlic cloves, finely minced
- 1 cup broccoli florets
- 1 cup cauliflowers
- 1/2-pound fresh mushrooms, sliced
- 4 green onions, cut into 1-inch pieces
- 2 tablespoons low-sodium soy sauce
- 3 tablespoon dry sherry
- 1 teaspoon finely minced fresh ginger
- 1 teaspoon cornstarch melted in 2 tablespoons water
- 1/4 teaspoon sesame oil
- 1/4 cup dry-roasted peanuts

 **PREPARATION** 10 MIN

 **COOKING** 30 MIN

 **SERVING** 6

DIRECTIONS

1. Cut off fat from chicken and thinly slice diagonally into 1-inch strips.
2. In a huge non-stick skillet, heat oil and stir-fry chicken 4 minutes Remove; put aside and keep warm.
3. Stir-fry garlic for 15 seconds; then broccoli and cauliflower, stir-fry 2 minutes. Then fry mushrooms, green onions, soy sauce, sherry and ginger for 2 minutes.
4. Pour dissolved arrowroot, sesame oil, peanuts and the chicken. Cook until heated through and sauce has thickened.

Nutritions: *256 calories, 9g carbohydrates, 30g protein*

94. ROSEMARY CHICKEN

INGREDIENTS

- 1 (2 1/2 to 3-pound) broiler-fryer chicken
- Salt and ground black pepper to taste
- 4 garlic cloves, finely minced
- 1 teaspoon dried rosemary
- 1/4 cup dry white wine
- 1/4 cup chicken broth

 **PREPARATION** 9 MIN    **COOKING** 30 MIN    **SERVING** 4

DIRECTIONS

1. Preheat broiler.
2. Season chicken with salt and pepper. Place in broiler pan. Broil 5 minutes per side.
3. Situate chicken, garlic, rosemary, wine and broth in a Dutch oven. Cook, covered, at medium heat about 30 minutes, turning once.

Nutritions: *176 Calories, 1g Carbohydrates, 1g Fat*

95. PEPPER CHICKEN SKILLET

INGREDIENTS

- 1 tablespoon vegetable oil
- 12 ounces skinless, boneless chicken breasts
- 2 garlic cloves, finely minced
- 3 bell peppers (red green and yellow)
- 2 medium onions, sliced
- 1 teaspoon ground cumin
- 1 1/2 teaspoon dried oregano leaves
- 2 teaspoons chopped fresh jalapeño peppers

- 3 tablespoons fresh lemon juice
- 2 tablespoons chopped fresh parsley
- 1/4 teaspoon salt

 **PREPARATION**
10 MIN

 **COOKING**
35 MIN

 **SERVING**
4

DIRECTIONS

1. In a big non-stick skillet, heat oil at medium-high heat; stir-fry chicken for 4 minutes.
2. Cook garlic for 15 seconds, stirring constantly. Fry bell pepper strips, sliced onion, cumin, oregano, and chilies for 2 to 3 minutes.
3. Toss lemon juice, parsley, salt and pepper and serve.

Nutritions: *174 Calories, 6g carbohydrate, 21g Protein*

96. DIJON SALMON

INGREDIENTS

- 1 tablespoon olive oil
- 1 1/2 pounds salmon fillets, cut into 6 pieces
- 1/4 cup lemon juice
- 2 tablespoons Equal (sugar substitute)
- 2 tablespoons Dijon mustard
- 1 tablespoon stick butter or margarine
- 1 tablespoon capers
- 1 clove garlic, minced
- 2 tablespoons chopped fresh dill

 **PREPARATION** 8 MIN

 **COOKING** 26 MIN

 **SERVING** 3

DIRECTIONS

1. Heat up olive oil in huge non-stick skillet over medium heat. Add salmon and cook 5 minutes, turning once. Reduce heat to medium-low; cover. Cook 6 to 8 minutes or until salmon flakes easily with a fork.
2. Remove salmon from skillet to serving plate; keep warm.
3. Add lemon juice, Equal, mustard, butter, capers and garlic to skillet. Cook at medium heat 3 minutes, stirring frequently.
4. To serve, spoon sauce over salmon. Sprinkle with dill.

Nutritions: *252 Calories, 2g carbohydrate, 23g Protein*

97. PULLED PORK

INGREDIENTS

- 1 whole pork tenderloin
- 1 tsp chili powder
- 1/2 tsp garlic powder
- 1/2 cup onion
- 1 1/2 teaspoons garlic
- 1 (14.5-ounce) can tomatoes
- 1 tablespoon cider vinegar
- 1 tablespoon prepared mustard
- 1 to 2 teaspoons chili powder
- 1/4 teaspoon maple extract

- 1/4 teaspoon liquid smoke
- 1/3 cup Equal (sugar substitute)
- 6 multigrain hamburger buns

 **PREPARATION**
10 MIN

 **COOKING**
35 MIN

 **SERVING**
4

DIRECTIONS

1. Season pork with 1 teaspoon chili powder and garlic powder; situate in baking pan. Bake in preheated 220°C oven 30 to 40 minutes. Set aside for 15 minutes. Slice into 2 to 3-inch slices; shred slices into bite-size pieces with a fork.
2. Coat medium saucepan with cooking spray. Cook onion and garlic for 5 minutes. Cook tomatoes, vinegar, mustard, chili powder, maple extract, and liquid smoke to saucepan. Allow to boil; decrease heat.
3. Simmer, uncovered, 10 to 15 minutes. Sprinkle Equal.
4. Season. Stir in pork into sauce. Cook 2 to 3 minutes. Spoon mixture into buns.

Nutritions: *252 Calories, 29g carbohydrate, 21g Protein*

98. HERB LEMON SALMON

INGREDIENTS

- 2 cups water
- 2/3 cup farro
- 1 medium eggplant
- 1 red bell pepper
- 1 summer squash
- 1 small onion
- 1½ cups cherry tomatoes
- 3 tablespoons extra-virgin olive oil
- ¾ teaspoon salt, divided
- ½ teaspoon ground pepper

- 2 tablespoons capers
- 1 tablespoon red-wine vinegar
- 2 teaspoons honey
- 1¼ pounds salmon cut into 4 portions
- 1 teaspoon lemon zest
- ½ teaspoon Italian seasoning
- Lemon wedges for serving

 **PREPARATION** 10 MIN  **COOKING** 27 MIN  **SERVING** 2

DIRECTIONS

1. Situate racks in upper and lower thirds of oven; set to 450°F. Prep 2 rimmed baking sheets with foil and coat with cooking spray.
2. Boil water and farro. Adjust heat to low, cover and simmer for 30 minutes. Drain if necessary.
3. Mix eggplant, bell pepper, squash, onion and tomatoes with oil, ½ teaspoon salt and ¼ teaspoon pepper. Portion between the baking sheets. Roast on the upper and lower racks, stir once halfway, for 25 minutes. Put them back to the bowl. Mix in capers, vinegar and honey.

4. Rub salmon with lemon zest, Italian seasoning and the remaining ¼ teaspoon each salt and pepper and situate on one of the baking sheets.
5. Roast on the lower rack for 12 minutes, depending on thickness. Serve with farro, vegetable caponata and lemon wedges.

Nutritions: *450 Calories, 17g fat, 41g carbohydrate*

99. GINGER CHICKEN

INGREDIENTS

- 2 tablespoons vegetable oil - divided use
- 1-pound boneless, skinless chicken breasts
- 1 cup red bell pepper strips
- 1 cup sliced fresh mushrooms
- 16 fresh pea pods, cut in half crosswise
- 1/2 cup sliced water chestnuts
- 1/4 cup sliced green onions

- 1 tablespoon grated fresh ginger root
- 1 large clove garlic, crushed
- 2/3 cup reduced-fat, reduced-sodium chicken broth
- 2 tablespoons Equal (sugar substitute)
- 2 tablespoons light soy sauce
- 4 teaspoons cornstarch
- 2 teaspoons dark sesame oil

 **PREPARATION** 10 MIN    **COOKING** 25 MIN   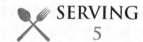 **SERVING** 5

DIRECTIONS

1. Heat up 1 tablespoon vegetable oil in huge skillet over medium-high heat. Stir fry chicken until no longer pink. Remove chicken from skillet.
2. Heat remaining 1 tablespoon vegetable oil in skillet. Add red peppers, mushrooms, pea pods, water chestnuts, green onion, ginger and garlic. Stir fry mixture 3 to 4 minutes until vegetables are crisp tender.
3. Meanwhile, combine chicken broth, Equal, soy sauce, cornstarch and sesame oil until smooth. Stir into skillet mixture. Cook at medium heat until thick and clear. Stir in chicken; heat through. Season with salt and pepper to taste, if desired.
4. Serve over hot cooked rice, if desired.

Nutritions: *263 Calories, 11g fat, 11g carbohydrate*

100. TERIYAKI CHICKEN

INGREDIENTS

- 1 tablespoon cornstarch
- 1 tablespoon cold water
- 1/2 cup Splenda
- 1/2 cup soy sauce
- 1/4 cup cider vinegar
- 1 clove garlic, minced
- 1/2 teaspoon ground ginger
- 1/4 teaspoon ground black pepper
- 12 skinless, boneless chicken breast halves

 **PREPARATION** 7 MIN

 **COOKING** 26 MIN

 **SERVING** 6

DIRECTIONS

1. In a small saucepan in low heat, mix cornstarch, cold water, Splenda, soy sauce, vinegar, garlic, ginger and ground black pepper. Let simmer, stirring frequently, until sauce thickens and bubbles.
2. Preheat oven to 425°F (220°C).
3. Position chicken pieces in a lightly greased 9x13 inch baking dish. Brush chicken with the sauce. Turn pieces over, and brush again.
4. Bake in the prepared oven for 30 minutes. Turn pieces over, and bake for another 30 minutes. Brush with sauce every 10 minutes during cooking.

Nutritions: *140 Calories, 3g carbohydrate, 25g Protein*

101. ROASTED GARLIC SALMON

INGREDIENTS

- 14 large cloves garlic
- ¼ cup olive oil
- 2 tablespoons fresh oregano
- 1 teaspoon salt
- ¾ teaspoon pepper
- 6 cups Brussels sprouts
- ¾ cup white wine, preferably Chardonnay
- 2 pounds wild-caught salmon fillet

 **PREPARATION** 8 MIN    **COOKING** 45 MIN    **SERVING** 6

DIRECTIONS

1. Prep oven at 450°F.
2. Finely chopped 2 garlic cloves and combine in a small bowl with oil, 1 tablespoon oregano, ½ teaspoon salt and ¼ teaspoon pepper. Slice remaining garlic and mix in Brussels sprouts and 3 tablespoons of the seasoned oil in a big roasting pan. Roast, stir once, for 15 minutes.
3. Pour in wine to the remaining oil mixture. Remove from oven, stir the vegetables and situate salmon on top. Dash with the wine mixture. Sprinkle with the remaining 1 tablespoon oregano and ½ teaspoon each salt and pepper.
4. Bake for 10 minutes more. Serve with lemon wedges.

Nutritions: *334 Calories, 10g carbohydrate, 33g Protein*

102. LEMON SESAME HALIBUT

INGREDIENTS

- 2 tablespoons lemon juice
- 2 tablespoons extra-virgin olive oil
- 1 clove garlic, minced
- Freshly ground pepper, to taste
- 2 tablespoons sesame seeds
- 1¼ pounds halibut, or mahi-mahi, cut into 4 portions
- 1½-2 teaspoons dried thyme leaves
- ¼ teaspoon coarse sea salt, or kosher salt

- Lemon wedges

 **PREPARATION** 9 MIN    **COOKING** 24 MIN   **SERVING** 4

DIRECTIONS

1. Preheat oven to 450°F. Line a baking sheet with foil.
2. Scourge lemon juice, oil, garlic and pepper in a shallow glass dish. Add fish and turn to coat. Wrap and marinate for 15 minutes.
3. Fry sesame seeds in a small dry skillet over medium-low heat, stirring constantly, for 3 minutes. Set aside to cool. Mix in thyme.
4. Season the fish with salt and coat evenly with the sesame seed mixture, covering the sides as well as the top. Transfer the fish to the prepared baking sheet and roast until just opaque in the center, 10 to 14 minutes. Serve with lemon wedges.

Nutritions: *225 Calories, 11g fat, 2g carbohydrate*

103. TURKEY SAUSAGE CASSEROLE

INGREDIENTS

- 5 ounces turkey breakfast sausage, casings removed
- 1 teaspoon canola oil
- 1 onion, chopped
- 1 red bell pepper, chopped
- 4 large eggs
- 4 large egg whites
- 2½ cups low-fat milk
- 1 teaspoon dry mustard
- ½ teaspoon salt
- ¼ teaspoon freshly ground pepper
- 2/3 cup low fat cheddar cheese, divided
- 10 slices white bread, crusts removed

 **PREPARATION** 12 MIN

 **COOKING** 32 MIN

 **SERVING** 4

DIRECTIONS

1. Grease 9-by-13-inch baking dish with cooking spray.
2. Fry sausage in a skillet over medium heat, crumbling with a fork, until browned. Transfer to a bowl.
3. Cook oil, onion and bell pepper to skillet; stirring occasionally, for 5 minutes. Fry sausage for 5 minutes more. Remove from heat and set aside.
4. Scourge eggs and egg whites in a large bowl until blended. Whisk in milk, mustard, salt and pepper. Stir in 1/3 cup cheddar.
5. Arrange bread in a single layer in prepared baking dish. Pour egg mixture over bread and top with reserved vegetables and sausage. Sprinkle with remaining 1/3 cup cheddar. Seal with plastic wrap and chill for at least 5 hours or overnight.
6. Preheat oven to 350°F. Bake casserole, uncovered, until set and puffed, 40 to 50 minutes. Serve hot.

Nutritions: *141 calories, 10g carbohydrates, 10g protein*

104. SPINACH CURRY

INGREDIENTS

- ¾ cup cooked whole-wheat angel hair pasta
- ½ cup baby spinach
- 1/3 cup chopped red bell pepper
- ¼ cup grated carrot
- ¼ cup chopped fresh cilantro
- 2 cups low-sodium chicken broth
- 1 tablespoon green curry paste

 **PREPARATION** 10 MIN  **COOKING** 22 MIN  **SERVING** 4

DIRECTIONS

1. Combine pasta, spinach, bell pepper, carrot and cilantro in a heatproof bowl.
2. Bring chicken broth to a boil. Stir in curry paste. Pour the broth over the pasta mixture. Serve hot.

Nutritions: *273 calories, 6g fiber, 45g carbohydrates*

105. ZUCCHINI HERB

INGREDIENTS

- 3 cups reduced-sodium chicken broth
- 1½ pounds zucchini,
- 1 tablespoon chopped fresh tarragon
- ¾ cup shredded reduced-fat Cheddar cheese
- ¼ teaspoon salt
- ¼ teaspoon freshly ground pepper

 **PREPARATION**
12 MIN

 **COOKING**
34 MIN

 **SERVING**
4

DIRECTIONS

1. Boil broth, zucchini and tarragon in a medium saucepan over high heat. Decrease heat to simmer and cook, uncovered, for 10 minutes. Puree in a blender until smooth.
2. Place soup back to the pan and heat over medium-high, slowly stirring in cheese until it is incorporated.
3. Remove from heat and season. Serve hot or chilled.

Nutritions: *110 calories, 2g fiber, 7g carbohydrates*

CHAPTER 5. SIDE DISH RECIPES

106. COFFEE-STEAMED CARROTS

INGREDIENTS

- 1 cup brewed coffee
- 1 teaspoon light brown sugar
- ½ teaspoon kosher salt
- Freshly ground black pepper
- 1-pound baby carrots
- Chopped fresh parsley
- 1 teaspoon grated lemon zest

 **PREPARATION**
10 MIN

 **COOKING**
3 MIN

 **SERVING**
4

DIRECTIONS

1. Pour the coffee into the electric pressure cooker. Stir in the brown sugar, salt, and pepper. Add the carrots.
2. Close the pressure cooker. Set to sealing.
3. Cook on high pressure for minutes.
4. Once complete, click Cancel and quick release the pressure.
5. Once the pin drops, open and remove the lid.
6. Using a slotted spoon, portion carrots to a serving bowl. Topped with the parsley and lemon zest, and serve.

Nutritions: *51 Calories, 12g Carbohydrates, 4g Fiber*

107. ROSEMARY POTATOES

INGREDIENTS

- 1lb red potatoes
- 1 cup vegetable stock
- 2tbsp olive oil
- 2tbsp rosemary sprigs

 **PREPARATION**
5 MIN

 **COOKING**
25 MIN

 **SERVING**
2

DIRECTIONS

1. Situate potatoes in the steamer basket and add the stock into the Instant Pot.
2. Steam the potatoes in your Instant Pot for 15 minutes.
3. Depressurize and pour away the remaining stock.
4. Set to sauté and add the oil, rosemary, and potatoes.
5. Cook until brown.

Nutritions: *195 Calories, 31g Carbohydrates, 1g Fat*

108. CORN ON THE COB

INGREDIENTS

- ·6 ears corn

 **PREPARATION**
10 MIN

 **COOKING**
5 MIN

 **SERVING**
12

DIRECTIONS

1. Take off husks and silk from the corn. Cut or break each ear in half.
2. Pour 1 cup of water into the bottom of the electric pressure cooker. Insert a wire rack or trivet.
3. Place the corn upright on the rack, cut-side down. Seal lid of the pressure cooker.
4. Cook on high pressure for 5 minutes.
5. When its complete, select Cancel and quick release the pressure.
6. When pin drops, unlock and take off lid.
7. Pull out the corn from the pot. Season as desired and serve immediately.

Nutritions: *62 Calories, 14g Carbohydrates, 1g Fiber*

109. CHILI LIME SALMON

INGREDIENTS

For Sauce:
- 1 jalapeno pepper
- 1 tablespoon chopped parsley
- 1 teaspoon minced garlic
- 1/2 teaspoon cumin
- 1/2 teaspoon paprika
- 1/2 teaspoon lime zest
- 1 tablespoon honey
- 1 tablespoon lime juice
- 1 tablespoon olive oil

- 1 tablespoon water

For Fish:
- 2 salmon fillets, each about 5 ounces
- 1 cup water
- 1/2 teaspoon salt
- 1/8 teaspoon ground black pepper

 **PREPARATION**
6 MIN

 **COOKING**
10 MIN

 **SERVING**
12

DIRECTIONS

1. Prepare salmon and for this, season salmon with salt and black pepper until evenly coated.
2. Plugin instant pot, insert the inner pot, pour in water, then place steamer basket and place seasoned salmon on it.
3. Seal instant pot with its lid, press the 'steam' button, then press the 'timer' to set the cooking time to 5 minutes and cook on high pressure, for 5 minutes.
4. Transfer all the ingredients for the sauce in a bowl, whisk until combined and set aside until required.
5. When the timer beeps, press 'cancel' button and do quick pressure release until pressure nob drops down.
6. Open the instant pot, then transfer salmon to a serving plate and drizzle generously with prepared sauce.
7. Serve straight away.

Nutritions: *305 Calories, 29g Carbohydrates, 6g Fiber*

110. COLLARD GREENS

INGREDIENTS

- 2 pounds chopped collard greens
- ¾ cup chopped white onion
- 1 teaspoon onion powder
- 1 teaspoon garlic powder
- 1 teaspoon salt
- 2 teaspoons brown sugar
- ½ teaspoon ground black pepper
- ½ teaspoon red chili powder
- ¼ teaspoon crushed red pepper flakes

- 3 tablespoons apple cider vinegar
- 2 tablespoons olive oil
- 14.5-ounce vegetable broth
- 1/2 cup water

 **PREPARATION** 5 MIN

 **COOKING** 6 H

 **SERVING** 12

DIRECTIONS

1. Plugin instant pot, insert the inner pot, add onion and collard and then pour in vegetable broth and water.
2. Close instant pot with its lid, seal, press the 'slow cook' button, then press the 'timer' to set the cooking time to 6 hours at high heat setting.
3. When the timer beeps, press 'cancel' button and do natural pressure release until pressure nob drops down.
4. Open the instant pot, add remaining ingredients and stir until mixed.
5. Then press the 'sauté/simmer' button and cook for 3 to minutes or more until collards reach to desired texture.
6. Serve straight away.

Nutritions: *49 Calories, 2.3g Carbohydrates, 0.5g Fiber*

111. MASHED PUMPKIN

INGREDIENTS

- 2 cups chopped pumpkin
- 0.5 cup water
- 2tbsp powdered sugar-free sweetener of choice
- 1tbsp cinnamont

 **PREPARATION**
9 MIN

 **COOKING**
15 MIN

 **SERVING**
2

DIRECTIONS

1. Place the pumpkin and water in your Instant Pot.
2. Seal and cook on Stew 15 minutes.
3. Remove and mash with the sweetener and cinnamon.

Nutritions: *12 Calories, 3g Carbohydrates, 1g Sugar*

112. PARMESAN-TOPPED ACORN SQUASH

INGREDIENTS

- 1 acorn squash (about 1 pound)
- 1 tablespoon extra-virgin olive oil
- 1 teaspoon dried sage leaves, crumbled
- ¼ teaspoon freshly grated nutmeg
- 1/8 teaspoon kosher salt
- 1/8 teaspoon freshly ground black pepper
- 2 tablespoons freshly grated Parmesan cheese

 **PREPARATION** 8 MIN    **COOKING** 20 MIN    **SERVING** 4

DIRECTIONS

1. Chop acorn squash in half lengthwise and remove the seeds. Cut each half in half for a total of 4 wedges. Snap off the stem if it's easy to do.
2. In a small bowl, combine the olive oil, sage, nutmeg, salt, and pepper. Brush the cut sides of the squash with the olive oil mixture.
3. Fill 1 cup of water into the electric pressure cooker and insert a wire rack or trivet.
4. Place the squash on the trivet in a single layer, skin-side down.
5. Set the lid of the pressure cooker on sealing.
6. Cook on high pressure for 20 minutes.
7. Once done, press Cancel and quick release the pressure.
8. Once the pin drops, open it.
9. Carefully remove the squash from the pot, sprinkle with the Parmesan, and serve.

Nutritions: 85 Calories, 12g Carbohydrates, 2g Fiber

113. QUINOA TABBOULEH

INGREDIENTS

- 1 cup quinoa, rinsed
- 1 large English cucumber
- 2 scallions, sliced
- 2 cups cherry tomatoes, halved
- 2/3 cup chopped parsley
- 1/2 cup chopped mint
- ½ teaspoon minced garlic
- 1/2 teaspoon salt
- ½ teaspoon ground black pepper
- 2 tablespoon lemon juice
- 1/2 cup olive oil

 **PREPARATION** 8 MIN    **COOKING** 16 MIN    **SERVING** 6

DIRECTIONS

1. Plugin instant pot, insert the inner pot, add quinoa, then pour in water and stir until mixed.
2. Close instant pot with its lid and turn the pressure knob to seal the pot.
3. Select 'manual' button, then set the 'timer' to 1 minute and cook in high pressure, it may take 7 minutes.
4. Once the timer stops, select 'cancel' button and do natural pressure release for 10 minutes and then do quick pressure release until pressure nob drops down.
5. Open the instant pot, fluff quinoa with a fork, then spoon it on a rimmed baking sheet, spread quinoa evenly and let cool.
6. Meanwhile, place lime juice in a small bowl, add garlic and stir until just mixed.
7. Then add salt, black pepper, and olive oil and whisk until combined.
8. Transfer cooled quinoa to a large bowl, add remaining ingredients, then drizzle generously with the prepared lime juice mixture and toss until evenly coated.
9. Taste quinoa to adjust seasoning and then serve.

Nutritions: *283 Calories, 30.6g Carbohydrates, 3.4g Fiber*

114. WILD RICE SALAD WITH CRANBERRIES AND ALMONDS

INGREDIENTS

For the rice
- 2 cups wild rice blend, rinsed
- 1 teaspoon kosher salt
- 2½ cups Vegetable Broth

For the dressing
- ¼ cup extra-virgin olive oil
- ¼ cup white wine vinegar
- 1½ teaspoons grated orange zest
- Juice of 1 medium orange (about ¼ cup)
- 1 teaspoon honey or pure maple syrup

For the salad
- ¾ cup unsweetened dried cranberries
- ½ cup sliced almonds, toasted
- Freshly ground black pepper

 **PREPARATION** 6 MIN

 **COOKING** 25 MIN

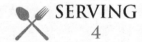 **SERVING** 4

DIRECTIONS

1. To make the rice
2. In the electric pressure cooker, combine the rice, salt, and broth.
3. Close and lock the lid. Set the valve to sealing.
4. Cook on high pressure for 25 minutes.
5. When the cooking is complete, hit Cancel and allow the pressure to release naturally for 1minutes, then quick release any remaining pressure.
6. Once the pin drops, unlock and remove the lid.
7. Let the rice cool briefly, then fluff it with a fork.
8. To make the dressing
9. While the rice cooks, make the dressing: In a small jar with a screw-top lid, combine the olive oil, vinegar, zest, juice, and honey. (If you don't have a jar, whisk the ingredients together in a small bowl.) Shake to combine.
10. To make the salad
11. Mix rice, cranberries, and almonds.
12. Add the dressing and season with pepper.
13. Serve warm or refrigerate.

Nutritions: 126 Calories, 18g Carbohydrates, 2g Fiber

115. LOW FAT ROASTIES

INGREDIENTS

- 1lb roasting potatoes
- 1 garlic clove
- 1 cup vegetable stock
- 2tbsp olive oil

 **PREPARATION** 8 MIN    **COOKING** 25 MIN    **SERVING** 2

DIRECTIONS

1. Position potatoes in the steamer basket and add the stock into the Instant Pot.
2. Steam the potatoes in your Instant Pot for 15 minutes.
3. Depressurize and pour away the remaining stock.
4. Set to sauté and add the oil, garlic, and potatoes. Cook until brown.

Nutritions: *201 Calories, 3g Carbohydrates, 6g Fat*

116. ROASTED PARSNIPS

INGREDIENTS

- 1lb parsnips
- 1 cup vegetable stock
- 2tbsp herbs
- 2tbsp olive oil

 **PREPARATION**
9 MIN

 **COOKING**
25 MIN

 **SERVING**
2

DIRECTIONS

1. Put the parsnips in the steamer basket and add the stock into the Instant Pot.
2. Steam the parsnips in your Instant Pot for 15 minutes.
3. Depressurize and pour away the remaining stock.
4. Set to sauté and add the oil, herbs and parsnips.
5. Cook until golden and crisp.

Nutritions: *130 Calories, 14g Carbohydrates, 4g Protein*

117. LOWER CARB HUMMUS

INGREDIENTS

- 0.5 cup dry chickpeas
- 1 cup vegetable stock
- 1 cup pumpkin puree
- 2tbsp smoked paprika
- salt and pepper to taste

 **PREPARATION**
9 MIN

 **COOKING**
60 MIN

 **SERVING**
2

DIRECTIONS

1. Soak the chickpeas overnight.
2. Place the chickpeas and stock in the Instant Pot.
3. Cook on Beans 60 minutes.
4. Depressurize naturally.
5. Blend the chickpeas with the remaining ingredients.

Nutritions: *135 Calories, 18g Carbohydrates, 3g Fat*

118. SWEET AND SOUR RED CABBAGE

INGREDIENTS

- 2 cups Spiced Pear Applesauce
- 1 small onion, chopped
- ½ cup apple cider vinegar
- ½ teaspoon kosher salt
- 1 head red cabbage

 **PREPARATION**
7 MIN

 **COOKING**
10 MIN

 **SERVING**
8

DIRECTIONS

1. In the electric pressure cooker, combine the applesauce, onion, vinegar, salt, and cup of water. Stir in the cabbage.
2. Seal lid of the pressure cooker.
3. Cook on high pressure for 10 minutes.
4. When the cooking is complete, hit Cancel and quick release the pressure.
5. Once the pin drops, unlock and remove the lid.
6. Spoon into a bowl or platter and serve.

Nutritions: *91 Calories, 18g Carbohydrates, 4g Fiber*

119. PINTO BEANS

INGREDIENTS

- 2 cups pinto beans, dried
- 1 medium white onion
- 1 ½ teaspoon minced garlic
- ¾ teaspoon salt
- 1/4 teaspoon ground black pepper
- 1 teaspoon red chili powder
- 1/4 teaspoon cumin
- 1 tablespoon olive oil
- 1 teaspoon chopped cilantro
- 5 ½ cup vegetable stock

 **PREPARATION** 6 MIN    **COOKING** 55 MIN    **SERVING** 10

DIRECTIONS

1. Plugin instant pot, insert the inner pot, press sauté/simmer button, add oil and when hot, add onion and garlic and cook for 3 minutes or until onions begin to soften.
2. Add remaining ingredients, stir well, then press the cancel button, shut the instant pot with its lid and seal the pot.
3. Click 'manual' button, then press the 'timer' to set the cooking time to 45 minutes and cook at high pressure.
4. Once done, click 'cancel' button and do natural pressure release for 10 minutes until pressure nob drops down.
5. Open the instant pot, spoon beans into plates and serve.

Nutritions: *107 Calories, 11.7g Carbohydrates, 4g Fiber*

120. PARMESAN CAULIFLOWER MASH

INGREDIENTS

- 1 head cauliflower
- ½ teaspoon kosher salt
- ½ teaspoon garlic pepper
- 2 tablespoons plain Greek yogurt
- ¾ cup freshly grated Parmesan cheese
- 1 tablespoon unsalted butter or ghee (optional)
- Chopped fresh chives

 **PREPARATION** 19 MIN  **COOKING** 5 MIN  **SERVING** 4

DIRECTIONS

1. Pour cup of water into the electric pressure cooker and insert a steamer basket or wire rack.
2. Place the cauliflower in the basket.
3. Cover lid of the pressure cooker to seal.
4. Cook on high pressure for 5 minutes.
5. Once complete, hit Cancel and quick release the pressure.
6. When the pin drops, remove the lid.
7. Remove the cauliflower from the pot and pour out the water. Return the cauliflower to the pot and add the salt, garlic pepper, yogurt, and cheese. Use an immersion blender to purée or mash the cauliflower in the pot.
8. Spoon into a serving bowl, and garnish with butter (if using) and chives.

Nutritions: *141 Calories, 12g Carbohydrates, 4g Fiber*

121. STEAMED ASPARAGUS

INGREDIENTS

- 1 lb. fresh asparagus, rinsed and tough ends trimmed
- 1 cup water

 **PREPARATION**
3 MIN

 **COOKING**
2 MIN

 **SERVING**
4

DIRECTIONS

1. Place the asparagus into a wire steamer rack, and set it inside your Instant Pot.
2. Add water to the pot. Close and seal the lid, turning the steam release valve to the "Sealing" position.
3. Select the "Steam" function to cook on high pressure for 2 minutes.
4. Once done, do a quick pressure release of the steam.
5. Lift the wire steamer basket out of the pot and place the asparagus onto a serving plate.
6. Season as desired and serve.

Nutritions: *22 Calories, 4g Carbohydrates, 2g Protein*

122. SQUASH MEDLEY

INGREDIENTS

- 2 lbs. mixed squash
- ½ cup mixed veg
- 1 cup vegetable stock
- 2 tbsps. olive oil
- 2 tbsps. mixed herbs

 **PREPARATION**
10 MIN

 **COOKING**
20 MIN

 **SERVING**
2

DIRECTIONS

1. Put the squash in the steamer basket and add the stock into the Instant Pot.
2. Steam the squash in your Instant Pot for 10 minutes.
3. Depressurize and pour away the remaining stock.
4. Set to sauté and add the oil and remaining ingredients.
5. Cook until a light crust form.

Nutritions: *100 Calories, 10g Carbohydrates, 6g Fat*

123. EGGPLANT CURRY

INGREDIENTS

- 3 cups chopped eggplant
- 1 thinly sliced onion
- 1 cup coconut milk
- 3 tbsps. curry paste
- 1 tbsp. oil or ghee

 **PREPARATION** 10 MIN

 **COOKING** 20 MIN

 **SERVING** 2

DIRECTIONS

1. Select Instant Pot to sauté and put the onion, oil, and curry paste.
2. Once the onion is soft, stir in remaining ingredients and seal.
3. Cook on Stew for 20 minutes. Release the pressure naturally.

Nutritions: *350 Calories, 15g Carbohydrates, 25g Fat*

124. LENTIL AND EGGPLANT STEW

INGREDIENTS

- 1 lb. eggplant
- 1 lb. dry lentils
- 1 cup chopped vegetables
- 1 cup low sodium vegetable broth

 **PREPARATION**
15 MIN

 **COOKING**
35 MIN

 **SERVING**
2

DIRECTIONS

1. Incorporate all the ingredients in your Instant Pot, cook on Stew for 35 minutes.
2. Release the pressure naturally and serve.

Nutritions: *310 Calories, 22g Carbohydrates, 10g Fat*

125. TOFU CURRY

INGREDIENTS

- 2 cups cubed extra firm tofu
- 2 cups mixed stir fry vegetables
- ½ cup soy yogurt
- 3 tbsps. curry paste
- 1 tbsp. oil or ghee

 **PREPARATION**
15 MIN

 **COOKING**
20 MIN

 **SERVING**
2

DIRECTIONS

1. Set the Instant Pot to sauté and add the oil and curry paste.
2. Once soft, place the remaining ingredients except for the yogurt and seal.
3. Cook on Stew for 20 minutes.
4. Release the pressure naturally and serve with a scoop of soy yogurt.

Nutritions: *300 Calories, 9g Carbohydrates, 14g Fat*

126. LENTIL AND CHICKPEA CURRY

INGREDIENTS

- 2 cups dry lentils and chickpeas
- 1 thinly sliced onion
- 1 cup chopped tomato
- 3 tbsps. curry paste
- 1 tbsp. oil or ghee

 **PREPARATION**
15 MIN

 **COOKING**
20 MIN

 **SERVING**
2

DIRECTIONS

1. Press Instant Pot to sauté and mix onion, oil, and curry paste.
2. Once the onion is cooked, stir the remaining ingredients and seal.
3. Cook on Stew for 20 minutes.
4. Release the pressure naturally and serve.

Nutritions: *360 Calories, 26g Carbohydrates, 19g Fat*

127. SPLIT PEA STEW

INGREDIENTS

- 1 cup dry split peas
- 1 lb. chopped vegetables
- 1 cup mushroom soup
- 2 tbsps. old bay seasoning

PREPARATION
5 MIN

COOKING
35 MIN

SERVING
2

DIRECTIONS

1. Incorporate all the ingredients in Instant Pot, cook for 33 minutes.
2. Release the pressure naturally.

Nutritions :300 Calories, 7g Carbohydrates, 2g Fat

128. KIDNEY BEAN STEW

INGREDIENTS

- 1 lb. cooked kidney beans
- 1 cup tomato passata
- 1 cup low sodium beef broth
- 3 tbsps. Italian herbs

 **PREPARATION**
15 MIN

 **COOKING**
15 MIN

 **SERVING**
2

DIRECTIONS

1. Incorporate all the ingredients in your Instant Pot, cook on Stew for 15 minutes.
2. Release the pressure naturally and serve.

Nutritions: *270 Calories, 16g Carbohydrates, 10g Fat*

129. FRIED TOFU HOTPOT

INGREDIENTS

- ½ lb. fried tofu
- 1 lb. chopped Chinese vegetable mix
- 1 cup low sodium vegetable broth
- 2 tbsps. 5 spice seasoning
- 1 tbsp. smoked paprika

 **PREPARATION**
15 MIN

 **COOKING**
15 MIN

 **SERVING**
2

DIRECTIONS

1. Combine all the ingredients in your Instant Pot, set on Stew for 15 minutes.
2. Release the pressure naturally and serve.

Nutritions: *320 Calories, 11g Carbohydrates, 23g Fat*

130. CHILI SIN CARNE

INGREDIENTS

- 3 cups mixed cooked beans
- 2 cups chopped tomatoes
- 1 tbsp. yeast extract
- 2 squares very dark chocolate
- 1 tbsp. red chili flakes

 **PREPARATION**
15 MIN

 **COOKING**
35 MIN

 **SERVING**
2

DIRECTIONS

1. Combine all the ingredients in your Instant Pot, cook for 35 minutes.
2. Release the pressure naturally and serve.

Nutritions: *240 Calories, 20g Carbohydrates, 3g Fat*

131. BRUSSELS SPROUTS

INGREDIENTS

- 1 tsp. extra-virgin olive oil
- 1 lb. halved Brussels sprouts
- 3 tbsps. apple cider vinegar
- 3 tbsps. gluten-free tamari soy sauce
- 3 tbsps. chopped sun-dried tomatoes

 **PREPARATION**
5 MIN

 **COOKING**
3 MIN

 **SERVING**
5

DIRECTIONS

1. Select the "Sauté" function on your Instant Pot, add oil and allow the pot to get hot.
2. Cancel the "Sauté" function and add the Brussels sprouts.
3. Stir well and allow the sprouts to cook in the residual heat for 2-3 minutes.
4. Add the tamari soy sauce and vinegar, and then stir.
5. Cover the Instant Pot, sealing the pressure valve by pointing it to "Sealing."
6. Select the "Manual, High Pressure" setting and cook for 3 minutes.
7. Once the cook cycle is done, do a quick pressure release, and then stir in the chopped sun-dried tomatoes.
8. Serve immediately.

Nutritions: *62 Calories, 10g Carbohydrates, 1g Fat*

132. GARLIC AND HERB CARROTS

INGREDIENTS

- 2 tbsps. butter
- 1 lb. baby carrots
- 1 cup water
- 1 tsp. fresh thyme or oregano
- 1 tsp. minced garlic
- Black pepper
- Coarse sea salt

 **PREPARATION**
2 MIN

 **COOKING**
18 MIN

 **SERVING**
3

DIRECTIONS

1. Fill water to the inner pot of the Instant Pot, and then put in a steamer basket.
2. Layer the carrots into the steamer basket.
3. Close and seal the lid, with the pressure vent in the "Sealing" position.
4. Select the "Steam" setting and cook for 2 minutes on high pressure.
5. Quick release the pressure and then carefully remove the steamer basket with the steamed carrots, discarding the water.
6. Add butter to the inner pot of the Instant Pot and allow it to melt on the "Sauté" function.
7. Add garlic and sauté for 30 seconds, and then add the carrots. Mix well.
8. Stir in the fresh herbs, and cook for 2-3 minutes.
9. Season with salt and black pepper, and the transfer to a serving bowl.
10. Serve warm and enjoy!

Nutritions: *122 Calories, 12g Carbohydrates, 7g Fat*

133. CILANTRO LIME DRUMSTICKS

INGREDIENTS

- 1 tbsp. olive oil
- 6 chicken drumsticks
- 4 minced garlic cloves
- ½ cup low-sodium chicken broth
- 1 tsp. cayenne pepper
- 1 tsp. crushed red peppers
- 1 tsp. fine sea salt
- Juice of 1 lime

To Serve:
- ·2 tbsp. chopped cilantro
- ·Extra lime zest

 **PREPARATION** 5 MIN

 **COOKING** 15 MIN

 **SERVING** 6

DIRECTIONS

1. Pour olive oil to the Instant Pot and set it on the "Sauté" function.
2. Once the oil is hot adding the chicken drumsticks, and season them well.
3. Using tongs, stir the drumsticks and brown the drumsticks for 2 minutes per side.
4. Add the lime juice, fresh cilantro, and chicken broth to the pot.
5. Lock and seal the lid, turning the pressure valve to "Sealing."
6. Cook the drumsticks on the "Manual, High Pressure" setting for 9 minutes.
7. Once done let the pressure release naturally.
8. Carefully transfer the drumsticks to an aluminum-foiled baking sheet and broil them in the oven for 3-5 minutes until golden brown.
9. Serve warm, garnished with more cilantro and lime zest.

Nutritions: *480 Calories, 3.3g Carbohydrates, 29g Fat*

134. EGGPLANT SPREAD

INGREDIENTS

- 4 tbsps. extra-virgin olive oil
- 2 lbs. eggplant
- 4 skin-on garlic cloves
- ½ cup water
- ¼ cup pitted black olives
- 3 sprigs fresh thyme
- Juice of 1 lemon
- 1 tbsp. tahini
- 1 tsp. sea salt
- Fresh extra-virgin olive oil

 **PREPARATION** 5 MIN    **COOKING** 18 MIN   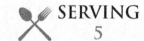 **SERVING** 5

DIRECTIONS

1. Peel the eggplant in alternating stripes, leaving some areas with skin and some with no skin.
2. Slice into big chunks and layer at the bottom of your Instant Pot.
3. Add olive oil to the pot, and on the "Sauté" function, fry and caramelize the eggplant on one side, about 5 minutes.
4. Add in the garlic cloves with the skin on.
5. Flip over the eggplant and then add in the remaining uncooked eggplant chunks, salt, and water.
6. Close the lid, ensure the pressure release valve is set to "Sealing."
7. Cook for 5 minutes on the "Manual, High Pressure" setting.
8. Once done, carefully open the pot by quick releasing the pressure through the steam valve.
9. Discard most of the brown cooking liquid.
10. Remove the garlic cloves and peel them.
11. Add the lemon juice, tahini, cooked and fresh garlic cloves and pitted black olives to the pot.
12. Using a hand-held immersion blender, process all the ingredients until smooth.
13. Pour out the spread into a serving dish and season with fresh thyme, whole black olives and some extra-virgin olive oil, prior to serving.

159 Nutritions: 155 Calories, 16.8g Carbohydrates, 11.7g Fat

135. CARROT HUMMUS

INGREDIENTS

- 1 chopped carrot
- 2 oz. cooked chickpeas
- 1 tsp. lemon juice
- 1 tsp. tahini
- 1 tsp. fresh parsley

 **PREPARATION**
15 MIN

 **COOKING**
10 MIN

 **SERVING**
2

DIRECTIONS

1. Place the carrot and chickpeas in your Instant Pot.
2. Add a cup of water, seal, cook for 10 minutes on Stew.
3. Depressurize naturally. Blend with the remaining ingredients.

Nutritions: *58 Calories, 8g Carbohydrates, 2g Fat*

136. VEGETABLE RICE PILAF

INGREDIENTS

- 1 tablespoon olive oil
- ½ medium yellow onion, diced
- 1 cup uncooked long-grain brown rice
- 2 cloves minced garlic
- ½ teaspoon dried basil
- Salt and pepper
- 2 cups fat-free chicken broth
- 1 cup frozen mixed veggies

 **PREPARATION**
5 MIN

 **COOKING**
25 MIN

 **SERVING**
6

DIRECTIONS

1. Cook oil in a large skillet over medium heat.
2. Add the onion and sauté for 3 minutes until translucent.
3. Stir in the rice and cook until lightly toasted.
4. Add the garlic, basil, salt, and pepper then stir to combined.
5. Stir in the chicken broth then bring to a boil.
6. Decrease heat and simmer, covered, for 10 minutes.
7. Stir in the frozen veggies then cover and cook for another 10 minutes until heated through. Serve hot.

Nutritions: *90 Calories, 12.6g Carbohydrates, 2.2g Fiber*

137. CURRY ROASTED CAULIFLOWER FLORETS

INGREDIENTS

- 8 cups cauliflower florets
- 2 tablespoons olive oil
- 1 teaspoon curry powder
- ½ teaspoon garlic powder
- Salt and pepper

 **PREPARATION**
5 MIN

 **COOKING**
25 MIN

 **SERVING**
6

DIRECTIONS

1. Prep the oven to 425°F and line a baking sheet with foil.
2. Toss the cauliflower with the olive oil and spread on the baking sheet.
3. Sprinkle with curry powder, garlic powder, salt, and pepper.
4. Roast for 25 minutes or until just tender. Serve hot.

Nutritions: *75 Calories, 7.4g Carbohydrates, 3.5g Fiber*

138. MUSHROOM BARLEY RISOTTO

INGREDIENTS

- 4 cups fat-free beef broth
- 2 tablespoons olive oil
- 1 small onion, diced well
- 2 cloves minced garlic
- 8 ounces thinly sliced mushrooms
- ¼ tsp dried thyme
- Salt and pepper
- 1 cup pearled barley
- ½ cup dry white wine

 **PREPARATION** 5 MIN  **COOKING** 25 MIN  **SERVING** 8

DIRECTIONS

1. Heat the beef broth in a medium saucepan and keep it warm.
2. Heat the oil in a large, deep skillet over medium heat.
3. Add the onions and garlic and sauté for 2 minutes then stir in the mushrooms and thyme.
4. Season with salt and pepper and sauté for 2 minutes more.
5. Add the barley and sauté for 1 minute then pour in the wine.
6. Ladle about ½ cup of beef broth into the skillet and stir well to combine.
7. Cook until most of the broth has been absorbed then add another ladle.
8. Repeat until you have used all of the broth and the barley is cooked to al dente.
9. Season and serve hot.

Nutritions: *155 Calories, 21.9g Carbohydrates, 4.4g Fiber*

139. BRAISED SUMMER SQUASH

INGREDIENTS

- 3 tablespoons olive oil
- 3 cloves minced garlic
- ¼ teaspoon crushed red pepper flakes
- 1-pound summer squash, sliced
- 1-pound zucchini, sliced
- 1 teaspoon dried oregano
- Salt and pepper

 **PREPARATION** 10 MIN

 **COOKING** 20 MIN

 **SERVING** 6

DIRECTIONS

1. Cook oil in a large skillet over medium heat.
2. Add the garlic and crushed red pepper and cook for 2 minutes.
3. Add the summer squash and zucchini and cook for 15 minutes, stirring often, until just tender.
4. Stir in the oregano then season with salt and pepper to taste. serve hot.

Nutritions: *90 Calories, 6.2g Carbohydrates, 1.8g Fiber*

140. GARLIC SAUTÉED SPINACH

INGREDIENTS

- 1 ½ tablespoons olive oil
- 4 cloves minced garlic
- 6 cups fresh baby spinach
- Salt and pepper

 **PREPARATION**
5 MIN

 **COOKING**
10 MIN

 **SERVING**
4

DIRECTIONS

1. Heat up oil in a huge skillet over medium-high heat.
2. Add the garlic and cook for 1 minute.
3. Stir in the spinach and season with salt and pepper.
4. Sauté for 1 to 2 minutes until just wilted. Serve hot.

Nutritions: *60 Calories, 2.6g Carbohydrates, 1.1g Fiber*

CHAPTER 6. DESSERT RECIPES

141. PUMPKIN & BANANA ICE CREAM

INGREDIENTS

- 15 oz. pumpkin puree
- 4 bananas, sliced and frozen
- 1 teaspoon pumpkin pie spice
- Chopped pecans

 **PREPARATION**
5 MIN

 **COOKING**
10 MIN

 **SERVING**
4

DIRECTIONS

1. Add pumpkin puree, bananas and pumpkin pie spice in a food processor.
2. Pulse until smooth.
3. Chill in the refrigerator.
4. Garnish with pecans.

Nutritions: *71 Calories, 18g Carbohydrate, 1.2g Protein*

142. BRULEE ORANGES

INGREDIENTS

- 4 oranges, sliced into segments
- 1 teaspoon ground cardamom
- 6 teaspoons brown sugar
- 1 cup nonfat Greek yogurt

 **PREPARATION**
5 MIN

 **COOKING**
10 MIN

 **SERVING**
4

DIRECTIONS

1. Preheat your broiler.
2. Arrange orange slices in a baking pan.
3. In a bowl, mix the cardamom and sugar.
4. Sprinkle mixture on top of the oranges. Broil for 5 minutes.
5. Serve oranges with yogurt.

Nutritions: *168 Calories, 26.9g Carbohydrate, 6.8g Protein*

143. FROZEN LEMON & BLUEBERRY

INGREDIENTS

- 6 cup fresh blueberries
- 8 sprigs fresh thyme
- ¾ cup light brown sugar
- 1 teaspoon lemon zest
- ¼ cup lemon juice
- 2 cups water

 **PREPARATION**
5 MIN

 **COOKING**
10 MIN

 **SERVING**
4

DIRECTIONS

1. Add blueberries, thyme and sugar in a pan over medium heat.
2. Cook for 6 to 8 minutes.
3. Transfer mixture to a blender.
4. Remove thyme sprigs.
5. Stir in the remaining ingredients.
6. Pulse until smooth.
7. Strain mixture and freeze for 1 hour.

Nutritions: *78 Calories, 20g Carbohydrate, 3g Protein*

144. PEANUT BUTTER CHOCO CHIP COOKIES

INGREDIENTS

- 1 egg
- ½ cup light brown sugar
- 1 cup natural unsweetened peanut butter
- Pinch salt
- ¼ cup dark chocolate chips

 **PREPARATION** 5 MIN    **COOKING** 10 MIN    **SERVING** 4

DIRECTIONS

1. Preheat your oven to 375 degrees F.
2. Mix egg, sugar, peanut butter, salt and chocolate chips in a bowl.
3. Form into cookies and place in a baking pan.
4. Bake the cookie for 10 minutes.
5. Let cool before serving.

Nutritions: *159 Calories, 12g Carbohydrate, 4.3g Protein*

145. WATERMELON SHERBET

INGREDIENTS

- 6 cups watermelon, sliced into cubes
- 14 oz. almond milk
- 1 tablespoon honey
- ¼ cup lime juice
- Salt to taste

 **PREPARATION**
5 MIN

 **COOKING**
3 MIN

 **SERVING**
4

DIRECTIONS

1. Freeze watermelon for 4 hours.
2. Add frozen watermelon and other ingredients in a blender.
3. Blend until smooth.
4. Transfer to a container with seal.
5. Seal and freeze for 4 hours.

Nutritions: *132 Calories, 24.5g Carbohydrate, 3.1g Protein*

146. STRAWBERRY & MANGO ICE CREAM

INGREDIENTS

- 8 oz. strawberries, sliced
- 12 oz. mango, sliced into cubes
- 1 tablespoon lime juice

 **PREPARATION**
5 MIN

 **COOKING**
10 MIN

 **SERVING**
4

DIRECTIONS

1. Add all ingredients in a food processor.
2. Pulse for 2 minutes.
3. Chill before serving.

Nutritions: *70 Calories, 17.4g Carbohydrate, 1.1g Protein*

147. SPARKLING FRUIT DRINK

INGREDIENTS

- 8 oz. unsweetened grape juice
- 8 oz. unsweetened apple juice
- 8 oz. unsweetened orange juice
- 1 qt. homemade ginger ale
- Ice

 **PREPARATION** 5 MIN    **COOKING** 10 MIN    **SERVING** 4

DIRECTIONS

1. Makes 7 servings. Mix first 4 ingredients together in a pitcher. Stir in ice cubes and 9 ounces of the beverage to each glass. Serve immediately.

Nutritions: *60 Calories, 1.1g Protein*

148. TIRAMISU SHOTS

INGREDIENTS

- 1 pack silken tofu
- 1 oz. dark chocolate, finely chopped
- ¼ cup sugar substitute
- 1 teaspoon lemon juice
- ¼ cup brewed espresso
- Pinch salt
- 24 slices angel food cake
- Cocoa powder (unsweetened)

 **PREPARATION**
5 MIN

 **COOKING**
10 MIN

 **SERVING**
4

DIRECTIONS

1. Add tofu, chocolate, sugar substitute, lemon juice, espresso and salt in a food processor.
2. Pulse until smooth.
3. Add angel food cake pieces into shot glasses.
4. Drizzle with the cocoa powder.
5. Pour the tofu mixture on top.
6. Top with the remaining angel food cake pieces.
7. Chill for 30 minutes and serve.

Nutritions: *75 Calories, 12g Carbohydrate, 2.9g Protein*

149. ICE CREAM BROWNIE CAKE

INGREDIENTS

- Cooking spray
- 12 oz. no-sugar brownie mix
- ¼ cup oil
- 2 egg whites
- 3 tablespoons water
- 2 cups sugar-free ice cream

 **PREPARATION** 5 MIN

 **COOKING** 10 MIN

 **SERVING** 4

DIRECTIONS

1. Preheat your oven to 325 degrees F.
2. Spray your baking pan with oil.
3. Mix brownie mix, oil, egg whites and water in a bowl.
4. Pour into the baking pan.
5. Bake for 25 minutes.
6. Let cool.
7. Freeze brownie for 2 hours.
8. Spread ice cream over the brownie.
9. Freeze for 8 hours.

Nutritions: *198 Calories, 33g Carbohydrate, 3g Protein*

150. PEANUT BUTTER CUPS

INGREDIENTS

- 1 packet plain gelatin
- ¼ cup sugar substitute
- 2 cups nonfat cream
- ½ teaspoon vanilla
- ¼ cup low-fat peanut butter
- 2 tablespoons unsalted peanuts, chopped

 **PREPARATION** 5 MIN

 **COOKING** 10 MIN

 **SERVING** 4

DIRECTIONS

1. Mix gelatin, sugar substitute and cream in a pan.
2. Let sit for 5 minutes.
3. Place over medium heat and cook until gelatin has been dissolved.
4. Stir in vanilla and peanut butter.
5. Pour into custard cups. Chill for 3 hours.
6. Top with the peanuts and serve.

Nutritions: *171 Calories, 21g Carbohydrate, 6.8g Protein*

151. FRUIT PIZZA

INGREDIENTS

- 1 teaspoon maple syrup
- ¼ teaspoon vanilla extract
- ½ cup coconut milk yogurt
- 2 round slices watermelon
- ½ cup blackberries, sliced
- ½ cup strawberries, sliced
- 2 tablespoons coconut flakes (unsweetened)

 **PREPARATION** 5 MIN  **COOKING** 10 MIN  **SERVING** 4

DIRECTIONS

1. Mix maple syrup, vanilla and yogurt in a bowl.
2. Spread the mixture on top of the watermelon slice.
3. Top with the berries and coconut flakes.

Nutritions: *70 Calories, 14.6g Carbohydrate, 1.2g Protein*

152. CHOCO PEPPERMINT CAKE

INGREDIENTS

- Cooking spray
- 1/3 cup oil
- 15 oz. package chocolate cake mix
- 3 eggs, beaten
- 1 cup water
- ¼ teaspoon peppermint extract

 **PREPARATION** 5 MIN    **COOKING** 10 MIN    **SERVING** 4

DIRECTIONS

1. Spray slow cooker with oil.
2. Mix all the ingredients in a bowl.
3. Use an electric mixer on medium speed setting to mix ingredients for 2 minutes.
4. Pour mixture into the slow cooker.
5. Cover the pot and cook on low for 3 hours.
6. Let cool before slicing and serving.

Nutritions: *185 Calories, 27g Carbohydrate, 3.8g Protein*

153. ROASTED MANGO

INGREDIENTS

- 2 mangoes, sliced
- 2 teaspoons crystallized ginger, chopped
- 2 teaspoons orange zest
- 2 tablespoons coconut flakes (unsweetened)

 **PREPARATION**
5 MIN

 **COOKING**
10 MIN

 **SERVING**
4

DIRECTIONS

1. Preheat your oven to 350 degrees F.
2. Add mango slices in custard cups.
3. Top with the ginger, orange zest and coconut flakes.
4. Bake in the oven for 10 minutes.

Nutritions: *89 Calories, 20g Carbohydrate, 0.8g Protein*

154. ROASTED PLUMS

INGREDIENTS

- Cooking spray
- 6 plums, sliced
- ½ cup pineapple juice (unsweetened)
- 1 tablespoon brown sugar
- 2 tablespoons brown sugar
- ¼ teaspoon ground cardamom
- ½ teaspoon ground cinnamon
- 1/8 teaspoon ground cumin

 **PREPARATION** 5 MIN    **COOKING** 10 MIN    **SERVING** 4

DIRECTIONS

1. Combine all the ingredients in a baking pan.
2. Roast in the oven at 450 degrees F for 20 minutes.

Nutritions: *102 Calories, 18.7g Carbohydrate, 2g Protein*

155. FIGS WITH HONEY & YOGURT

INGREDIENTS

- ½ teaspoon vanilla
- 8 oz. nonfat yogurt
- 2 figs, sliced
- 1 tablespoon walnuts, chopped and toasted
- 2 teaspoons honey

 **PREPARATION**
5 MIN

 **COOKING**
10 MIN

 **SERVING**
4

DIRECTIONS

1. Stir vanilla into yogurt.
2. Mix well.
3. Top with the figs and sprinkle with walnuts.
4. Drizzle with honey and serve.

Nutritions: *157 Calories, 24g Carbohydrate, 7g Protein*

156. FLOURLESS CHOCOLATE CAKE

INGREDIENTS

- ½ Cup of stevia
- 12 Ounces of unsweetened baking chocolate
- 2/3 Cup of ghee
- 1/3 Cup of warm water
- ¼ Teaspoon of salt
- 4 Large pastured eggs
- 2 Cups of boiling water

 **PREPARATION** 10 MIN

 **COOKING** 45 MIN

 **SERVING** 6

DIRECTIONS

1. Line the bottom of a 9-inch pan of a spring form with a parchment paper.
2. Heat the water in a small pot; then add the salt and the stevia over the water until wait until the mixture becomes completely dissolved.
3. Melt the baking chocolate into a double boiler or simply microwave it for about 30 seconds.
4. Mix the melted chocolate and the butter in a large bowl with an electric mixer.
5. Beat in your hot mixture; then crack in the egg and whisk after adding each of the eggs.
6. Pour the obtained mixture into your prepared spring form tray.
7. Wrap the spring form tray with a foil paper.
8. Place the spring form tray in a large cake tray and add boiling water right to the outside; make sure the depth doesn't exceed 1 inch.
9. Bake the cake into the water bath for about 45 minutes at a temperature of about 350 F.
10. Remove the tray from the boiling water and transfer to a wire to cool.
11. Let the cake chill for an overnight in the refrigerator.

Nutritions: *295 Calories, 6g Carbohydrates, 4g Fiber*

157. RASPBERRY CAKE WITH WHITE CHOCOLATE SAUCE

INGREDIENTS

- 5 Ounces of melted cacao butter
- 2 Ounces of grass-fed ghee
- ½ Cup of coconut cream
- 1 Cup of green banana flour
- 3 Teaspoons of pure vanilla
- 4 Large eggs
- ½ Cup of as Lakanto Monk Fruit
- 1 Teaspoon of baking powder
- 2 Teaspoons of apple cider vinegar
- 2 Cup of raspberries

For white chocolate sauce:
- 3 and ½ ounces of cacao butter
- ½ Cup of coconut cream
- 2 Teaspoons of pure vanilla extract
- 1 Pinch of salt

 **PREPARATION** 15 MIN

 **COOKING** 60 MIN

 **SERVING** 5

DIRECTIONS

1. Preheat your oven to a temperature of about 280 degrees Fahrenheit.
2. Combine the green banana flour with the pure vanilla extract, the baking powder, the coconut cream, the eggs, the cider vinegar and the monk fruit and mix very well.
3. Leave the raspberries aside and line a cake loaf tin with a baking paper.
4. Pour in the batter into the baking tray and scatter the raspberries over the top of the cake.
5. Place the tray in your oven and bake it for about 60 minutes; in the meantime, prepare the sauce by

Directions for sauce:

6. Combine the cacao cream, the vanilla extract, the cacao butter and the salt in a saucepan over a low heat.
7. Mix all your ingredients with a fork to make sure the cacao butter mixes very well with the cream.
8. Remove from the heat and set aside to cool a little bit; but don't let it harden.
9. Drizzle with the chocolate sauce.
10. Scatter the cake with more raspberries.
11. Slice your cake; then serve and enjoy it!

Nutritions: 323 Calories, 9.9g Carbohydrates, 4g Fiber

158. LAVA CAKE

INGREDIENTS

- 2 Oz of dark chocolate; you should at least use chocolate of 85% cocoa solids
- 1 Tablespoon of super-fine almond flour
- 2 Oz of unsalted almond butter
- 2 Large eggs

 **PREPARATION** 10 MIN    **COOKING** 10 MIN    **SERVING** 2

DIRECTIONS

1. Heat your oven to a temperature of about 350 Fahrenheit.
2. Grease 2 heat proof ramekins with almond butter.
3. Now, melt the chocolate and the almond butter and stir very well.
4. Beat the eggs very well with a mixer.
5. Add the eggs to the chocolate and the butter mixture and mix very well with almond flour and the swerve; then stir.
6. Pour the dough into 2 ramekins.
7. Bake for about 9 to 10 minutes.
8. Turn the cakes over plates and serve with pomegranate seeds!

Nutritions: *459 Calories, 3.5g Carbohydrates, 0.8g Fiber*

159. CHEESE CAKE

INGREDIENTS

For Almond Flour Cheesecake Crust:
- 2 Cups of Blanched almond flour
- 1/3 Cup of almond Butter
- 3 Tablespoons of Erythritol (powdered or granular)
- 1 Teaspoon of Vanilla extract

- 3 Large Eggs
- 1 Tablespoon of Lemon juice
- 1 Teaspoon of Vanilla extract

For Keto Cheesecake Filling:
- 32 Oz of softened Cream cheese
- 1 and ¼ cups of powdered erythritol

 **PREPARATION** 5 MIN    **COOKING** 45 MIN    **SERVING** 4

DIRECTIONS

1. Preheat your oven to a temperature of about 350 degrees F.
2. Grease a spring form pan of 9¨ with cooking spray or just line its bottom with a parchment paper.
3. In order to make the cheesecake rust, stir in the melted butter, the almond flour, the vanilla extract and the erythritol in a large bowl.
4. The dough will get will be a bit crumbly; so, press it into the bottom of your prepared tray.
5. Bake for about 12 minutes; then let cool for about 10 minutes.
6. In the meantime, beat the softened cream cheese and the powdered sweetener at a low speed until it becomes smooth.
7. Crack in the eggs and beat them in

at a low to medium speed until it becomes fluffy. Make sure to add one a time.
8. Add in the lemon juice and the vanilla extract and mix at a low to medium speed with a mixer.
9. Pour your filling into your pan right on top of the crust. You can use a spatula to smooth the top of the cake.
10. Bake for about 45 to 50 minutes.
11. Remove the baked cheesecake from your oven and run a knife around its edge.
12. Let the cake cool for about 4 hours in the refrigerator.
13. Serve and enjoy your delicious cheese cake!

Nutritions: *325 Calories, 6g Carbohydrates, 1g Fiber*

160. CAKE WITH WHIPPED CREAM ICING

INGREDIENTS

- ¾ Cup Coconut flour
- ¾ Cup of Swerve Sweetener
- ½ Cup of Cocoa powder
- 2 Teaspoons of Baking powder
- 6 Large Eggs
- 2/3 Cup of Heavy Whipping Cream
- ½ Cup of Melted almond Butter

- ¼ Cup of Swerve Sweetener
- 1 Teaspoon of Vanilla extract
- 1/3 Cup of Sifted Cocoa Powder

For whipped Cream Icing:
- 1 Cup of Heavy Whipping Cream

 **PREPARATION** 20 MIN

 **COOKING** 25 MIN

 **SERVING** 7

DIRECTIONS

1. Pre-heat your oven to a temperature of about 350 F.
2. Grease an 8x8 cake tray with cooking spray.
3. Add the coconut flour, the Swerve sweetener; the cocoa powder, the baking powder, the eggs, the melted butter; and combine very well with an electric or a hand mixer.
4. Pour your batter into the cake tray and bake for about 25 minutes.
5. Remove the cake tray from the oven and let cool for about 5 minutes.

For the Icing
6. Whip the cream until it becomes fluffy; then add in the Swerve, the vanilla and the cocoa powder.
7. Add the Swerve, the vanilla and the cocoa powder; then continue mixing until your ingredients are very well combined.
8. Frost your baked cake with the icing!

Nutritions: *357 Calories, 11g Carbohydrates, 2g Fiber*

161. WALNUT-FRUIT CAKE

INGREDIENTS

- 1/2 Cup of almond butter (softened)
- ¼ Cup of so Nourished granulated erythritol
- 1 Tablespoon of ground cinnamon
- ½ Teaspoon of ground nutmeg
- ¼ Teaspoon of ground cloves
- 4 Large pastured eggs
- 1 Teaspoon of vanilla extract
- ½ Teaspoon of almond extract
- 2 Cups of almond flour
- ½ Cup of chopped walnuts
- ¼ Cup of dried of unsweetened cranberries
- ¼ Cup of seedless raisins

 **PREPARATION** 15 MIN    **COOKING** 20 MIN    **SERVING** 7

DIRECTIONS

1. Preheat your oven to a temperature of about 350 F and grease an 8-inch baking tin of round shape with coconut oil.
2. Beat the granulated erythritol on a high speed until it becomes fluffy.
3. Add the cinnamon, the nutmeg, and the cloves; then blend your ingredients until they become smooth.
4. Crack in the eggs and beat very well by adding one at a time, plus the almond extract and the vanilla.
5. Whisk in the almond flour until it forms a smooth batter then fold in the nuts and the fruit.
6. Spread your mixture into your prepared baking pan and bake it for about 20 minutes.
7. Remove the cake from the oven and let cool for about 5 minutes.
8. Dust the cake with the powdered erythritol.

Nutritions: *250 Calories, 12g Carbohydrates, 2g Fiber*

162. GINGER CAKE

INGREDIENTS

- ½ Tablespoon of unsalted almond butter to grease the pan
- 4 Large eggs
- ¼ Cup coconut milk
- 2 Tablespoons of unsalted almond butter
- 1 and ½ teaspoons of stevia
- 1 Tablespoon of ground cinnamon
- 1 Tablespoon of natural cocoa powder
- 1 Tablespoon of fresh ground ginger
- ½ Teaspoon of kosher salt
- 1 and ½ cups of blanched almond flour
- ½ Teaspoon of baking soda

 **PREPARATION** 15 MIN

 **COOKING** 20 MIN

 **SERVING** 9

DIRECTIONS

1. Preheat your oven to a temperature of 325 F.
2. Grease a glass baking tray of about 8X8 inches generously with almond butter.
3. In a large bowl, whisk all together the coconut milk, the eggs, the melted almond butter, the stevia, the cinnamon, the cocoa powder, the ginger and the kosher salt.
4. Whisk in the almond flour, then the baking soda and mix very well.
5. Pour the batter into the prepared pan and bake for about 20 to 25 minutes.
6. Let the cake cool for about 5 minutes.

Nutritions: *175 Calories, 5g Carbohydrates, 1.9g Fiber*

163. ORANGE CAKE

INGREDIENTS

- 2 and ½ cups of almond flour
- 2 Unwaxed washed oranges
- 5 Large separated eggs
- 1 Teaspoon of baking powder
- 2 Teaspoons of orange extract
- 1 Teaspoon of vanilla bean powder
- 6 Seeds of cardamom pods crushed
- 16 drops of liquid stevia; about 3 teaspoons
- 1 Handful of flaked almonds to decorate

 **PREPARATION** 10 MIN

 **COOKING** 50 MIN

 **SERVING** 8

DIRECTIONS

1. Preheat your oven to a temperature of about 350 Fahrenheit.
2. Line a rectangular bread baking tray with a parchment paper.
3. Place the oranges into a pan filled with cold water and cover it with a lid.
4. Bring the saucepan to a boil, then let simmer for about 1 hour and make sure the oranges are totally submerged.
5. Make sure the oranges are always submerged to remove any taste of bitterness.
6. Cut the oranges into halves; then remove any seeds; and drain the water and set the oranges aside to cool down.
7. Cut the oranges in half and remove any seeds, then puree it with a blender or a food processor.
8. Separate the eggs; then whisk the egg whites until you see stiff peaks forming.
9. Add all your ingredients except for the egg whites to the orange mixture and add in the egg whites; then mix.
10. Pour the batter into the cake tin and sprinkle with the flaked almonds right on top.
11. Bake your cake for about 50 minutes.
12. Remove the cake from the oven and set aside to cool for 5 minutes.

Nutritions: *164 Calories, 7.1g Carbohydrates, 2.7g Fiber*

164. LEMON CAKE

INGREDIENTS

- 2 Medium lemons
- 4 Large eggs
- 2 Tablespoons of almond butter
- 2 Tablespoons of avocado oil
- 1/3 cup of coconut flour
- 4-5 tablespoons of honey (or another sweetener of your choice)
- ½ tablespoon of baking soda

 **PREPARATION** 20 MIN

 **COOKING** 20 MIN

 **SERVING** 9

DIRECTIONS

1. Preheat your oven to a temperature of about 350 F.
2. Crack the eggs in a large bowl and set two egg whites aside.
3. Whisk the 2 whites of eggs with the egg yolks, the honey, the oil, the almond butter, the lemon zest and the juice and whisk very well together.
4. Combine the baking soda with the coconut flour and gradually add this dry mixture to the wet ingredients and keep whisking for a couple of minutes.
5. Beat the two eggs with a hand mixer and beat the egg into foam.
6. Add the white egg foam gradually to the mixture with a silicone spatula.
7. Transfer your obtained batter to tray covered with a baking paper.
8. Bake your cake for about 20 to 22 minutes.
9. Let the cake cool for 5 minutes; then slice your cake.

Nutritions: *164 Calories, 7.1g Carbohydrates, 2.7g Fiber*

165. CINNAMON CAKE

INGREDIENTS

For Cinnamon Filling:
- 3 Tablespoons of Swerve Sweetener
- 2 Teaspoons of ground cinnamon

For the Cake:
- 3 Cups of almond flour
- ¾ Cup of Swerve Sweetener
- ¼ Cup of unflavored whey protein powder
- 2 Teaspoon of baking powder
- ½ Teaspoon of salt
- 3 large pastured eggs
- ½ Cup of melted coconut oil

- ½ Teaspoon of vanilla extract
- ½ Cup of almond milk
- 1 Tablespoon of melted coconut oil

For cream cheese Frosting:
- 3 Tablespoons of softened cream cheese
- 2 Tablespoons of powdered Swerve Sweetener
- 1 Tablespoon of coconut heavy whipping cream
- ½ Teaspoon of vanilla extract
-

 **PREPARATION** 15 MIN    **COOKING** 35 MIN    **SERVING** 8

DIRECTIONS

1. Preheat your oven to a temperature of about 325 F and grease a baking tray of 8x8 inch.
2. For the filling, mix the Swerve and the cinnamon in a mixing bowl and mix very well; then set it aside.
3. For the preparation of the cake; whisk all together the almond flour, the sweetener, the protein powder, the baking powder, and the salt in a mixing bowl.
4. Add in the eggs, the melted coconut oil and the vanilla extract and mix very well.
5. Add in the almond milk and keep stirring until your ingredients are very well combined.
6. Spread about half of the batter in the prepared pan; then sprinkle with about two thirds of the filling mixture.
7. Spread the remaining mixture of the batter over the filling and smooth it with a spatula.
8. Bake for about 35 minutes in the oven.
9. Brush with the melted coconut oil and sprinkle with the remaining cinnamon filling.
10. Prepare the frosting by beating the cream cheese, the powdered erythritol, the cream and the vanilla extract in a mixing bowl until it becomes smooth.
11. Drizzle frost over the cooled cake.

Nutritions: 222 Calories, 5.4g Carbohydrates, 1.5g Fiber

166. MADELEINE

INGREDIENTS

- 2 Large pastured eggs
- ¾ Cup of almond flour
- 1 and ½ Tablespoons of Swerve
- ¼ Cup of cooled, melted coconut oil
- 1 Teaspoon of vanilla extract
- 1 Teaspoon of almond extract
- 1 Teaspoon of lemon zest
- ¼ Teaspoon of salt

 **PREPARATION** 10 MIN    **COOKING** 15 MIN    **SERVING** 12

DIRECTIONS

1. Preheat your oven to a temperature of about 350 F.
2. Combine the eggs with the salt and whisk on a high speed for about 5 minutes.
3. Slowly add in the Swerve and keep mixing on high for 2 additional minutes.
4. Stir in the almond flour until it is very well-incorporated; then add in the vanilla and the almond extracts.
5. Add in the melted coconut oil and stir all your ingredients together.
6. Pour the obtained batter into equal parts in a greased Madeleine tray.
7. Bake your Ketogenic Madeleine for about 13 minutes or until the edges start to have a brown color.
8. Flip the Madeleines out of the baking tray.

Nutritions: *87 Calories, 3g Carbohydrates, 3g Fiber*

167. WAFFLES

INGREDIENTS

For Ketogenic waffles:
- 8 Oz of cream cheese
- 5 Large pastured eggs
- 1/3 Cup of coconut flour
- ½ Teaspoon of Xanthan gum
- 1 Pinch of salt
- ½ Teaspoon of vanilla extract
- 2 Tablespoons of Swerve
- ¼ Teaspoon of baking soda
- 1/3 Cup of almond milk

Optional ingredients:
- ½ Teaspoon of cinnamon pie spice
- ¼ Teaspoon of almond extract

For low-carb Maple Syrup:
- 1 Cup of water
- 1 Tablespoon of Maple flavor
- ¾ Cup of powdered Swerve
- 1 Tablespoon of almond butter
- ½ Teaspoon of Xanthan gum

 **PREPARATION** 20 MIN  **COOKING** 30 MIN 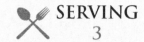 **SERVING** 3

DIRECTIONS

For the waffles:
1. Make sure all your ingredients are exactly at room temperature.
2. Place all your ingredients for the waffles from cream cheese to pastured eggs, coconut flour, Xanthan gum, salt, vanilla extract, the Swerve, the baking soda and the almond milk except for the almond milk with the help of a processor.
3. Blend your ingredients until it becomes smooth and creamy; then transfer the batter to a bowl.
4. Add the almond milk and mix your ingredients with a spatula.
5. Heat a waffle maker to a temperature of high.
6. Spray your waffle maker with coconut oil and add about ¼ of the batter in it evenly with a spatula into your waffle iron.
7. Close your waffle and cook until you get the color you want.
8. Carefully remove the waffles to a platter.

For the Ketogenic Maple Syrup:
9. 9.   Place 1 and ¼ cups of water, the swerve and the maple in a small pan and bring to a boil over a low heat; then let simmer for about 10 minutes.
10. 10. Add the coconut oil.
11. 11.   Sprinkle the Xanthan gum over the top of the waffle and use an immersion blender to blend smoothly.
12. 12. Serve and enjoy your delicious waffles!

193 **Nutritions:** *316 Calories, 7g Carbohydrates, 3g Fiber*

168. PRETZELS

INGREDIENTS

- 1 and ½ cups of pre-shredded mozzarella
- 2 Tablespoons of full fat cream cheese
- 1 Large egg
- ¾ Cup of almond flour+ 2 tablespoons of ground almonds or almond meal
- ½ Teaspoon of baking powder
- 1 Pinch of coarse sea salt

 **PREPARATION** 10 MIN    **COOKING** 20 MIN    **SERVING** 8

DIRECTIONS

1. Heat your oven to a temperature of about 180 C/356 F.
2. Melt the cream cheese and the mozzarella cheese and stir over a low heat until the cheeses are perfectly melted.
3. If you choose to microwave the cheese, just do that for about 1 minute no more and if you want to do it on the stove, turn off the heat as soon as the cheese is completely melted.
4. Add the large egg to the prepared warm dough; then stir until your ingredients are very well combined. If the egg is cold; you will need to heat it gently.
5. Add in the ground almonds or the almond flour and the baking powder and stir until your ingredients are very well combined.
6. Take one pinch of the dough of cheese and toll it or stretch it in your hands until it is about 18 to 20 cm of length; if your dough is sticky, you can oil your hands to avoid that.
7. Now, form pretzels from the cheese dough and nicely shape it; then place it over a baking sheet.
8. Sprinkle with a little bit of salt and bake for about 17 minutes.

Nutritions: *113 Calories, 2.5g Carbohydrates, 0.8g Fiber*

169. CHEESY TACO BITES

INGREDIENTS

- 2 Cups of Packaged Shredded Cheddar Cheese
- 2 Tablespoon of Chili Powder
- 2 Tablespoons of Cumin
- 1 Teaspoon of Salt
- 8 Teaspoons of coconut cream for garnishing
- Use Pico de Gallo for garnishing as well

 **PREPARATION** 5 MIN    **COOKING** 10 MIN    **SERVING** 2

DIRECTIONS

1. Preheat your oven to a temperature of about 350 F.
2. Over a baking sheet lined with a parchment paper, place 1 tablespoon piles of cheese and make sure to a space of 2 inches between each.
3. Place the baking sheet in your oven and bake for about 5 minutes.
4. Remove from the oven and let the cheese cool down for about 1 minute; then carefully lift up and press each into the cups of a mini muffin tin.
5. Make sure to press the edges of the cheese to form the shape of muffins mini.
6. Let the cheese cool completely; then remove it.
7. While you continue to bake the cheese and create your cups.
8. Fill the cheese cups with the coconut cream, then top with the Pico de Gallo.

Nutritions: *73 Calories, 3g Carbohydrates, 4g Protein*

170. NUT SQUARES

INGREDIENTS

- 2 Cups of almonds, pumpkin seeds, sunflower seeds and walnuts
- ½ Cup of desiccated coconut
- 1 Tablespoon of chia seeds
- ¼ Teaspoon of salt
- 2 Tablespoons of coconut oil
- 1 Teaspoon of vanilla extract
- 3 Tablespoons of almond or peanut butter
- 1/3 Cup of Sukrin Gold Fiber Syrup

 **PREPARATION** 30 MIN    **COOKING** 10 MIN    **SERVING** 10

DIRECTIONS

1. Line a square baking tin with a baking paper; then lightly grease it with cooking spray
2. Chop all the nuts roughly; then slightly grease it too, you can also leave them as whole
3. Mix the nuts in a large bowl; then combine them in a large bowl with the coconut, the chia seeds and the salt
4. In a microwave-proof bowl; add the coconut oil; then add the vanilla, the coconut butter or oil, the almond butter and the fiber syrup and microwave the mixture for about 30 seconds
5. Stir your ingredients together very well; then pour the melted mixture right on top of the nuts
6. Press the mixture into your prepared baking tin with the help of the back of a measuring cup and push very well
7. Freeze your treat for about 1 hour before cutting it
8. Cut your frozen nut batter into small cubes or squares of the same size

Nutritions: *268 Calories, 14g Carbohydrates, 1g Fiber*

CHAPTER 7.
JUICE AND SMOOTHIE RECIPES

171. CHOCO-NUT MILKSHAKE

INGREDIENTS

- 2 cups unsweetened coconut, almond
- 1 banana, sliced and frozen
- ¼ cup unsweetened coconut flakes
- 1 cup ice cubes
- ¼ cup macadamia nuts, chopped
- 3 tablespoons sugar-free sweetener
- 2 tablespoons raw unsweetened cocoa powder
- Whipped coconut cream

 **PREPARATION** 10 MIN    **COOKING** 0 MIN    **SERVING** 2

DIRECTIONS

1. Place all ingredients into a blender and blend on high until smooth and creamy.
2. Divide evenly between 4 "mocktail" glasses and top with whipped coconut cream, if desired.
3. Add a cocktail umbrella and toasted coconut for added flair.
4. Enjoy your delicious Choco-nut smoothie!

Nutritions: *12g Carbohydrates, 3g Protein, 199 Calories*

172. PINEAPPLE & STRAWBERRY SMOOTHIE

INGREDIENTS

- 1 cup strawberries
- 1 cup pineapple, chopped
- ¾ cup almond milk
- 1 tablespoon almond butter

 **PREPARATION**
7 MIN

 **COOKING**
0 MIN

 **SERVING**
2

DIRECTIONS

1. Add all ingredients to a blender.
2. Blend until smooth.
3. Add more almond milk until it reaches your desired consistency.
4. Chill before serving.

Nutritions: *255 Calories, 39g Carbohydrate, 5.6g Protein*

173. CANTALOUPE SMOOTHIE

INGREDIENTS

- ¾ cup carrot juice
- 4 cups cantaloupe, sliced into cubes
- Pinch of salt
- Frozen melon balls
- Fresh basil

 **PREPARATION**
11 MIN

 **COOKING**
0 MIN

 **SERVING**
2

DIRECTIONS

1. Add the carrot juice and cantaloupe cubes to a blender. Sprinkle with salt.
2. Process until smooth.
3. Transfer to a bowl.
4. Chill in the refrigerator for at least 30 minutes.
5. Top with the frozen melon balls and basil before serving.

Nutritions: *135 Calories, 31g Carbohydrate, 3.4g Protein*

174. BERRY SMOOTHIE WITH MINT

INGREDIENTS

- ¼ cup orange juice
- ½ cup blueberries
- ½ cup blackberries
- 1 cup reduced-fat plain kefir
- 1 tablespoon honey
- 2 tablespoons fresh mint leaves

 **PREPARATION**
7 MIN

 **COOKING**
0 MIN

 **SERVING**
2

DIRECTIONS

1. Add all the ingredients to a blender.
2. Blend until smooth.

Nutritions: *137 Calories, 27g Carbohydrate, 6g Protein*

175. GREEN SMOOTHIE

INGREDIENTS

- 1 cup vanilla almond milk (unsweetened)
- ¼ ripe avocado, chopped
- 1 cup kale, chopped
- 1 banana
- 2 teaspoons honey
- 1 tablespoon chia seeds
- 1 cup ice cubes

 **PREPARATION** 10 MIN
 **COOKING** 0 MIN
 **SERVING** 2

DIRECTIONS

1. Combine all the ingredients in a blender.
2. Process until creamy.

Nutritions: *343 Calories, 14.7g Carbohydrate, 5.9g Protein*

176. BANANA, CAULIFLOWER & BERRY SMOOTHIE

INGREDIENTS

- 2 cups almond milk (unsweetened)
- 1 cup banana, sliced
- ½ cup blueberries
- ½ cup blackberries
- 1 cup cauliflower rice
- 2 teaspoons maple syrup

 **PREPARATION**
9 MIN

 **COOKING**
0 MIN

 **SERVING**
2

DIRECTIONS

1. Pour almond milk into a blender.
2. Stir in the rest of the ingredients.
3. Process until smooth.
4. Chill before serving.

Nutritions: *149 Calories, 29g Carbohydrate, 3g Protein*

177. BERRY & SPINACH SMOOTHIE

INGREDIENTS

- 2 cups strawberries
- 1 cup raspberries
- 1 cup blueberries
- 1 cup fresh baby spinach leaves
- 1 cup pomegranate juice
- 3 tablespoons milk powder (unsweetened)

 **PREPARATION** 11 MIN
 **COOKING** 0 MIN
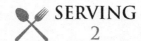 **SERVING** 2

DIRECTIONS

1. Mix all the ingredients in a blender.
2. Blend until smooth.
3. Chill before serving.

Nutritions: *118 Calories, 25.7g Carbohydrate, 4.6g Protein*

178. PEANUT BUTTER SMOOTHIE WITH BLUEBERRIES

INGREDIENTS

- 2 tablespoons creamy peanut butter
- 1 cup vanilla almond milk (unsweetened)
- 6 oz. soft silken tofu
- ½ cup grape juice
- 1 cup blueberries
- Crushed ice

 **PREPARATION** 12 MIN

 **COOKING** 0 MIN

 **SERVING** 2

DIRECTIONS

1. Mix all the ingredients in a blender.
2. Process until smooth.

Nutritions: *247 Calories, 30g Carbohydrate, 10.7g Protein*

179. PEACH & APRICOT SMOOTHIE

INGREDIENTS

- 1 cup almond milk (unsweetened)
- 1 teaspoon honey
- ½ cup apricots, sliced
- ½ cup peaches, sliced
- ½ cup carrot, chopped
- 1 teaspoon vanilla extract

 **PREPARATION**
11 MIN

 **COOKING**
0 MIN

 **SERVING**
2

DIRECTIONS

1. Mix milk and honey.
2. Pour into a blender.
3. Add the apricots, peaches and carrots.
4. Stir in the vanilla.
5. Blend until smooth.

Nutritions: *153 Calories, 30g Carbohydrate, 32.6g Protein*

180. TROPICAL SMOOTHIE

INGREDIENTS

- 1 banana, sliced
- 1 cup mango, sliced
- 1 cup pineapple, sliced
- 1 cup peaches, sliced
- 6 oz. nonfat coconut yogurt
- Pineapple wedges

 **PREPARATION** 8 MIN    **COOKING** 0 MIN    **SERVING** 2

DIRECTIONS

1. Freeze the fruit slices for 1 hour.
2. Transfer to a blender.
3. Stir in the rest of the ingredients except pineapple wedges.
4. Process until smooth.
5. Garnish with pineapple wedges.

Nutritions: *102 Calories, 22.6g Carbohydrate, 2.5g Protein*

181. BANANA & STRAWBERRY SMOOTHIE

INGREDIENTS

- 1 banana, sliced
- 4 cups fresh strawberries, sliced
- 1 cup ice cubes
- 6 oz. yogurt
- 1 kiwi fruit, sliced

 **PREPARATION** 7 MIN    **COOKING** 0 MIN    **SERVING** 2

DIRECTIONS

1. Add banana, strawberries, ice cubes and yogurt in a blender.
2. Blend until smooth.
3. Garnish with kiwi fruit slices and serve.

Nutritions: *54 Calories, 11.8g Carbohydrate, 1.7g Protein*

182. CANTALOUPE & PAPAYA SMOOTHIE

INGREDIENTS

- ¾ cup low-fat milk
- ½ cup papaya, chopped
- ½ cup cantaloupe, chopped
- ½ cup mango, cubed
- 4 ice cubes
- Lime zest

 **PREPARATION**
9 MIN

 **COOKING**
0 MIN

 **SERVING**
2

DIRECTIONS

1. Pour milk into a blender.
2. Add the chopped fruits and ice cubes.
3. Blend until smooth.
4. Garnish with lime zest and serve.

Nutritions: *207 Calories, 18.4g Carbohydrate, 7.7g Protein*

183. WATERMELON & CANTALOUPE SMOOTHIE

INGREDIENTS

- 2 cups watermelon, sliced
- 1 cup cantaloupe, sliced
- ½ cup nonfat yogurt
- ¼ cup orange juice

 **PREPARATION** 10 MIN    **COOKING** 0 MIN    **SERVING** 2

DIRECTIONS

1. Add all the ingredients to a blender.
2. Blend until creamy and smooth.
3. Chill before serving.

Nutritions: 114 Calories, 13g Carbohydrate, 4.8g Protein

184. RASPBERRY AND PEANUT BUTTER SMOOTHIE

INGREDIENTS

- Peanut butter, smooth and natural [2 tbsp]
- Skim milk [2 tbsp]
- Raspberries, fresh [1 or 1 ½ cups]
- Ice cubes [1 cup]
- Stevia [2 tsp]

 **PREPARATION**
10 MIN

 **COOKING**
0 MIN

 **SERVING**
2

DIRECTIONS

1. Situate all the ingredients in your blender. Set the mixer to puree. Serve.

Nutritions: *170 Calories, 8.6g Fat, 20g Carbohydrate*

185. STRAWBERRY, KALE AND GINGER SMOOTHIE

INGREDIENTS

- Curly kale leaves, fresh and large with stems removed [6 pcs]
- Grated ginger, raw and peeled [2 tsp]
- Water, cold [½ cup]
- Lime juice [3 tbsp]
- Honey [2 tsp]
- Strawberries, fresh and trimmed [1 or 1 ½ cups]
- Ice cubes [1 cup]

 **PREPARATION**
13 MIN

 **COOKING**
0 MIN

 **SERVING**
2

DIRECTIONS

1. Position all the ingredients in your blender. Set to puree. Serve.

Nutritions: *205 Calories, 2.9g Fat, 42.4g Carbohydrates*

CHAPTER 8. INFUSIONS AND HERBAL TEA RECIPES

186. LEMON ROOIBOS ICED TEA

INGREDIENTS

- 4 bags natural, unflavored rooibos tea
- 4 cups boiling water
- 3 tablespoons freshly squeezed lemon juice
- 30–40 drops liquid stevia

 **PREPARATION** 10 MIN    **COOKING** 0 MIN    **SERVING** 4

DIRECTIONS

1. Situate tea bags into tea pot and pour the boiling water over the bags.
2. Set aside to room temperature, then refrigerate the tea until it is ice-cold.
3. Remove the tea bags. Squeeze them gently.
4. Add the lemon juice and liquid stevia to taste and stir until well mixed.
5. Serve immediately, preferably with ice cubes and some nice garnishes, like lemon wedges.

Nutritions: 70 Calories, 16g Carbohydrates, 1g Protein

187. LEMON LAVENDER ICED TEA

INGREDIENTS

- 2 bags natural, unflavored rooibos tea
- 2 oz lemon chunks without peel and pith, seeds removed
- 1 teaspoon dried lavender blossoms placed in a tea ball
- 4 cups water, at room temperature
- 20–40 drops liquid stevia

 **PREPARATION**
15 MIN

 **COOKING**
0 MIN

 **SERVING**
4

DIRECTIONS

1. Place the tea bags, lemon chunks and the tightly-closed tea ball with the lavender blossoms in a 1.5 qt (1.5 l) pitcher.
2. Pour in the water.
3. Refrigerate overnight.
4. Remove the tea bags, lemon chunks and the tea ball with the lavender on the next day. Squeeze the tea bags gently to save as much liquid as possible.
5. Add liquid stevia to taste and stir until well mixed.
6. Serve immediately with ice cubes and lemon wedges.

Nutritions: *81 Calories, 12g Carbohydrates, 3g Protein*

188. CHERRY VANILLA ICED TEA

INGREDIENTS

- 4 bags natural, unflavored rooibos tea
- 4 cups boiling water
- 2 tablespoons freshly squeezed lime juice
- 1–2 tablespoons cherry flavoring
- 30–40 drops (or to taste) liquid vanilla stevia

 **PREPARATION** 12 MIN

 **COOKING** 0 MIN

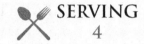 **SERVING** 4

DIRECTIONS

1. Place tea bags into tea pot and pour the boiling water over the bags.
2. Put aside the tea cool down first, then refrigerate the tea until it is ice-cold.
3. Remove the tea bags. Squeeze them lightly.
4. Add the lime juice, cherry flavoring and the vanilla stevia and stir until well mixed.
5. Serve immediately, preferably with ice cubes and some nice garnishes like lime wedges and fresh cherries.

Nutritions: *89 Calories, 14g Carbohydrates, 2g Protein*

189. ELEGANT BLUEBERRY ROSE WATER ICED TEA

INGREDIENTS

- 2 bags herbal blueberry tea
- 4 cups boiling water
- 20 drops liquid stevia
- 1 tablespoon rose water

 **PREPARATION** 12 MIN    **COOKING** 0 MIN    **SERVING** 4

DIRECTIONS

1. Position tea bags into tea pot and pour the boiling water over the bags.
2. Allow tea cool down first, then refrigerate the tea until it is ice-cold.
3. Remove the tea bags. Press them gently.
4. Add the liquid stevia and the rose water and stir until well mixed.
5. Serve immediately, preferably with ice cubes and some nice garnishes, like fresh blueberries or natural rose petals

Nutritions: *75 Calories, 10g Carbohydrates, 2g Protein*

190. MELBA ICED TEA

INGREDIENTS

- 1 bag herbal raspberry tea
- 1 bag herbal peach tea
- 4 cups boiling water
- 10 drops liquid peach stevia
- 20–40 drops (or to taste) liquid vanilla stevia

 **PREPARATION** 10 MIN

 **COOKING** 0 MIN

 **SERVING** 4

DIRECTIONS

1. Pour the boiling water over the tea bags.
2. Leave tea cool down on room temperature, then refrigerate the tea until it is ice-cold.
3. Remove the tea bags. Press lightly.
4. Add the peach stevia and stir until well mixed.
5. Add vanilla stevia to taste and stir until well mixed.
6. Serve immediately, preferably with ice cubes and some nice garnishes, like vanilla bean, fresh raspberries or peach slices.

Nutritions: *81 Calories, 14g Carbohydrates, 4g Protein*

191. MERRY RASPBERRY CHERRY ICED TEA

INGREDIENTS

- 2 bags herbal raspberry tea
- 4 cups boiling water
- 1 teaspoon stevia-sweetened cherry-flavored drink mix
- 1 teaspoon freshly squeezed lime juice
- 10–20 drops (or to taste) liquid stevia

 **PREPARATION** 11 MIN

 **COOKING** 0 MIN

 **SERVING** 4

DIRECTIONS

1. Put the tea bags into tea pot and fill in boiling water over the bags.
2. Let the tea cool down first to room temperature, then chill until it is ice-cold.
3. Discard tea bags. Squeeze them.
4. Add the cherry-flavored drink mix and the lime juice and stir until the drink mix is dissolved.
5. Add liquid stevia to taste and stir until well mixed.
6. Serve immediately, preferably with ice cubes or crushed ice and some nice garnishes, like fresh raspberries and cherries.

Nutritions: *82 Calories, 11g Carbohydrates, 4g Protein*

192. VANILLA KISSED PEACH ICED TEA

INGREDIENTS

- 2 bags herbal peach tea
- 4 cups boiling water
- 1 teaspoon vanilla extract
- 1 teaspoon freshly squeezed lemon juice
- 30–40 drops (or to taste) liquid stevia

 **PREPARATION**
13 MIN

 **COOKING**
0 MIN

 **SERVING**
4

DIRECTIONS

1. Soak tea bags over boiling water.
2. Allow to cool down on room temperature, then refrigerate the tea until it is ice-cold.
3. Remove and press tea bags.
4. Add the vanilla extract and the lemon juice and stir until well mixed.
5. Add liquid stevia to taste and stir until well mixed.
6. Serve immediately, preferably with ice cubes and some nice garnishes, like peach slices.

Nutritions: *88 Calories, 14g Carbohydrates, 3g Protein*

193. XTREME BERRIED ICED TEA

INGREDIENTS

- 2 bags herbal Wild Berry Tea
- 4 cups = 950 ml boiling water
- 2 teaspoons freshly squeezed lime juice
- 40 drops berry-flavored liquid stevia
- 10 drops (or to taste) liquid stevia

 **PREPARATION** 10 MIN    **COOKING** 0 MIN    **SERVING** 4

DIRECTIONS

1. Submerge tea bags into boiling water.
2. Set aside to cool down, then refrigerate the tea until it is ice-cold.
3. Pull out tea bags. Squeeze.
4. Add the lime juice and the berry stevia and stir until well mixed.
5. Add liquid stevia to taste and stir until well mixed.
6. Serve immediately.

Nutritions: *76 Calories, 14g Carbohydrates, 4g Protein*

194. REFRESHINGLY PEPPERMINT ICED TEA

INGREDIENTS

- 4 bags peppermint tea
- 4 cups = 950 ml boiling water
- 2 teaspoons stevia-sweetened lime-flavored drink mix
- 1 cup = 240 ml ice-cold sparkling water

 **PREPARATION** 15 MIN  **COOKING** 0 MIN  **SERVING** 5

DIRECTIONS

1. Immerse tea bags on boiling water.
2. Set aside before cooling until it is ice-cold.
3. Take out tea bags then press.
4. Add the lime-flavored drink mix and stir until it is properly dissolved.
5. Add the sparkling water and stir very gently.
6. Serve immediately, preferably with ice cubes, mint leaves and lime wedges.

Nutritions: *78 Calories, 17g Carbohydrates, 4g Protein*

195. LEMONGRASS MINT ICED TEA

INGREDIENTS

- 1 stalk lemongrass, chopped in 1-inch
- 1/2 cup chopped, loosely packed mint sprigs
- 4 cups boiling water

 **PREPARATION** 12 MIN

 **COOKING** 0 MIN

 **SERVING** 4

DIRECTIONS

1. Put the lemongrass and the mint into tea pot and pour the boiling water over them.
2. Let cool down first to room temperature, then refrigerate until the tea is ice-cold.
3. Filter out the lemongrass and the mint.
4. Add liquid vanilla stevia to taste if you prefer some sweetness and stir until well mixed.
5. Serve immediately, preferably with ice cubes and some nice garnishes, like mint sprigs and lemongrass stalks.

Nutritions: *89 Calories, 17g Carbohydrates, 5g Protein*

196. SPICED TEA

INGREDIENTS

- 2 bags Bengal Spice tea
- 2 teaspoons freshly squeezed lemon juice
- 1 packet zero-carb vanilla stevia
- 1 packet zero-carb stevia
- 4 cups boiling water

 **PREPARATION**
8 MIN

 **COOKING**
0 MIN

 **SERVING**
4

DIRECTIONS

1. Put the tea bags, lemon juice and the both stevia into tea pot.
2. Pour in the boiling water.
3. Put aside to cool over room temperature, then refrigerate.
4. Pull away tea bags then squeeze it.
5. Stir gently.
6. Serve immediately, preferably with ice cubes or crushed ice and some lemon wedges or slices.

Nutritions: *91 Calories, 16g Carbohydrates, 1g Protein*

197. INFUSED PUMPKIN SPICE LATTE

INGREDIENTS

- 2 cups almond milk
- ¼ cup coconut cream
- 2 teaspoons cannabis coconut oil
- ¼ cup pure pumpkin, canned
- ½ teaspoon vanilla extract
- 1 ½ teaspoon pumpkin spice
- ½ cup coconut whipped cream
- 1 pinch of salt

 **PREPARATION** 1 MIN    **COOKING** 0 MIN    **SERVING** 2

DIRECTIONS

1. Place all ingredients except the coconut whipped cream, in pan over a medium low heat stove.
2. Whisk well and allow to simmer but don't boil!
3. Simmer for about 5 minutes.
4. Pour into mugs and serve.

Nutritions: *94 Calories, 17g Carbohydrates, 3g Protein*

198. INFUSED TURMERIC-GINGER TEA

INGREDIENTS

- 1 cup water
- ½ cup coconut milk
- 1 teaspoon cannabis oil
- ½ teaspoon ground turmeric
- ¼ cup fresh ginger root, sliced
- 1 pinch Stevia or maple syrup, to taste

 **PREPARATION** 9 MIN    **COOKING** 0 MIN    **SERVING** 1

DIRECTIONS

1. Combine all ingredients in a small saucepan over medium heat.
2. Heat until simmer and turn heat low.
3. Take pan off the heat after 2 minutes
4. Let it cool, strain mixture into cup or mug.

Nutritions: *98 Calories, 14g Carbohydrates, 2g Protein*

199. INFUSED LONDON FOG

INGREDIENTS

- 1 cup hot water
- 1 Earl Grey teabag
- 1 teaspoon cannabis coconut oil
- ¼ cup almond milk
- ¼ teaspoon vanilla extract
- 1 pinch Stevia or sugar, to taste

 **PREPARATION** 17 MIN    **COOKING** 0 MIN    **SERVING** 2

DIRECTIONS

1. Fill up half a mug with boiling water.
2. Add teabag; if you prefer your tea strong, add two.
3. Add cannabis oil and stir well.
4. Add almond milk to fill your mug and stir through with the vanilla extract
5. Use Stevia or sugar to sweeten your Earl Grey to taste.

Nutritions: *76 Calories, 14g Carbohydrates, 2g Protein*

200. INFUSED CRANBERRY-APPLE SNUG

INGREDIENTS

- ½ cup fresh cranberry juice
- ½ cup fresh apple juice, cloudy
- ½ stick cinnamon
- 2 whole cloves
- ¼ lemon, sliced
- 1 pinch of Stevia or sugar, to taste
- cranberries for garnish (optional)

 **PREPARATION**
10 MIN

 **COOKING**
0 MIN

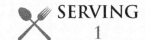 **SERVING**
1

DIRECTIONS

1. Combine all ingredients in a small saucepan over medium heat.
2. Heat until simmer and turn heat low.
3. Let it cool, strain the mixture into a mug.
4. Serve with cinnamon stick and cranberries in a mug.

Nutritions: *88 Calories, 15g Carbohydrates, 3g Protein*

CONCLUSION

A stationary lifestyle is one in which you sit a large portion of the day and embrace minimal physical activity. The connection between inactive conduct and the danger of diabetes is simply demonstrated.

Physical exercise expands the insulin affectability of cells when you exercise; less insulin is required to empower your blood glucose to enter your cells. Numerous physical movement types decrease blood glucose levels in pre-diabetic grown-ups who are stout or overweight, counting vigorous exercise, quality preparing, and high-power stretch preparation.

One study of pre-diabetics showed that high-force exercise expanded insulin effectively by 85% while tolerable extreme exercise expanded it by over half. However, this impact just occurred when they worked out.

To improve insulin reaction in pre-diabetics, they expected to consume in any event 2,000 calories per week through exercise. That isn't too difficult to think about doing if you set your focus on it. Try to locate a physical action you appreciate and usually embrace and stick to it as long as possible.

Quit smoking, other than tumors of the lung, breast, prostate, colon, throat, and stomach related tract, just as emphysema and coronary illness, has proven connections between smoking (and introduction to recycled smoke) and type 2 diabetes.

Smoking builds the danger of diabetes

by 44% in regular smokers and 61% in overwhelming smokers (more than 20 cigarettes every day), contrasted with non-smokers as per a meta-investigation of a few studies that together secured more than one million smokers.

Stopping smoking diminishes this hazard after some time, but not right away. Most individuals who develop type 2 diabetes are overweight or hefty. Also, individuals with pre-diabetes will, in general, have visceral fat, i.e., they haul their excess weight around their center and stomach organs, for example, the liver.

Studies have demonstrated that increased visceral fat advances insulin opposition, expanding the danger of diabetes significantly. This hazard can be diminished by shedding pounds, particularly around the center.

One investigation of more than 1,000 individuals found that for each kilogram (2.2 lbs.) they lost; their danger of diabetes was decreased by 16%. This examination found that the most extreme decrease of a hazard was 96%, i.e., lost 6 kilograms (13.2 lbs.).

There are numerous sound ways of shedding pounds by exercise and dieting.

You have numerous dietary alternatives to browse Mediterranean, paleo, low-carb, vegan. The best, maybe, is the Beating-Diabetes diet.

Reduce the fat in your diet. As you know,

the primary driver of type 2 diabetes is fat sticking up the receptors in your muscle cells, so the insulin can't open the cell films to permit glucose to enter. The "fix" is to unblock the receptors.

As you are pre-diabetic, fat is now starting to gum up the receptors. You can unblock the receptors by limiting the fat you ingest in your diet.

To limit the fat you eat: Make sure that under 10% of the content in any food you eat originates from fat (read the marks) and Reduce your utilization of meat, eggs, and dairy items, as reasonable and center around foods dependent on plants (products of the soil).

You can't change your past conduct, your age, or even your qualities. However, you can manage to improve your lifestyle, what you eat and drink, and how you take care of yourself.

Made in the USA
Monee, IL
13 March 2021